LIBBY LANGDON'S
Small Space Solutions

*Secrets for Making Any Room Look Elegant
and Feel Spacious on Any Budget*

LIBBY LANGDON

Guilford, Connecticut
An imprint of The Globe Pequot Press

To buy books in quantity for corporate use
or incentives, call **(800) 962–0973**
or e-mail **premiums@GlobePequot.com.**

MAKE IT EASY

Knack is a registered trademark of Morris Publishing Group, LLC, and is used with express permission.

Text designed by Sheryl P. Kober

All photos courtesy of Libby Langdon and Noël Sutherland
Noël Sutherland Photography/www.noelsutherland.com

Library of Congress Cataloging-in-Publication Data is available on file.

ISBN 978-1-59921-424-5

Printed in the United States of America

10 9 8 7 6 5 4 3 2 1

This book is dedicated to my Mom and Dad, Mary Ann, and Fran, who gave me an opportunity at a young age to follow my dreams, find my voice, and spread my wings. Their ever-present love and support has allowed me to live many lives, re-create myself, and discover what I want to do and who I want to be. The ease in which they've taught me their incredibly positive outlook and enthusiasm for life has been inspirational, and I take that glass-half-full attitude with me everywhere I go. They created a warm and wonderful home for me to grow up in, filled with lots of style, love, and laughter, so it's a natural path for me to want to help people create that for themselves. I will never be able to repay them for all they've done, but I will be able to take the gifts they've shared with me and pass them along to others who might need them.

I also dedicate this to my late grandmother, Chickie, who got my imagination of "what could possibly be" up and running. She was a writer, teacher, volunteer, who had plenty of sass, wit, and showmanship, and the twinkle in her eye always let you know fun was just around the corner. She was strong willed and she was a survivor, yet her creative spirit taught me to believe in magic places where truly incredible things could happen.

Contents

Libby's Tricks of the Trade

Libby's Note to the Reader

Hey! It's so fantastic you picked up my book. You probably want to know what this book is all about. I have so much I want to tell you! First, some questions. Do you live in a small space? Do you want some fresh design ideas and inspiration that won't cost you an arm and a leg? Do you want great tips on how to make your space function as well as how to make it look beautiful? (It must seem weird that I'm asking all these questions, because you can't answer me. And even if you did answer me, I am not where you are right now, so I wouldn't really be able to hear you.) Okay, at this point if you're still reading, you might think I'm a little crazy, but you also must be looking for some hard-and-fast information that you can use to create the space you envision yourself living in and loving. I just so happen to know how to help you do that!

Maybe you love your bedroom, but you can't get a sense on how to make your living room work; or your kitchen area is great, and you really hate the vibe of your bedroom. I'll help you identify and rectify the problems by figuring out what you like and don't like as well as encourage you to think about the room in your home that you like the least (you know the room that made you go into the interior design section of the bookstore and look for some solutions in the first place) and how to convert it into your favorite room! It's not all about starting from scratch (unless you want to) but more how to transform, rework, and incorporate your existing furnishings into your new design scheme as well as add some simple solutions to update your overall look.

You'll see that this book is chock-full of things you can do yourself to make changes to your home that will work whether you're in a tiny studio apartment, a compact condo, or a little house (or you just want some cool, cost-conscious ways to create your own chic space). You won't need a custom carpenter or loads of cash to implement my ideas, which range from ways to visually trick the eye and make your rooms seem larger, to easily incorporating systems of storage and organization that will let you capitalize on the space you do have. In addition to helpful hints, there are loads of great pictures that will illustrate, illuminate, and inspire the redesign of your space (some of them aren't teeny-tiny spaces, but I believe you'll be able to use the images as a springboard to discover the best way to announce your own personal style).

Take a flip through of what I have in store for you. I think interior design should be fun, easy, and accessible. Most of all I want to give you the tools, support, and encouragement to design the most beautiful, comfortable, and practical house that you can call home no matter how small it is! I've really loved our time together just now; let's do this again real soon; you're so much fun! I feel like I've done all the talking . . . now it's time for you to read whichever chapters speak to your most urgent small-space interior design needs and get cracking on your small space!

Libby

INTRODUCTION

When someone tells you that he or she lives in a small house or apartment, it often conjures up negative images of a cramped, cluttered, or confining space. But as America's leading small-space designer, I'm here to buck the system and change that stereotype: Dimensions only define the size of a room or home, *not* its style. Armed with some basic design knowledge and some of my tricks of the trade, you can create a gracious, inviting small-space home that is also extremely functional. Great design comes in all shapes and sizes; I've seen lots of fabulous small spaces that are chic and stylish, and I've also seen some enormous homes that feel cold and have no style whatsoever. It's not just whether your home is big or small—it's all a matter of what you do with what you have!

Another common misconception about small spaces is that they only apply to people living in city apartments, but I can assure you that I have seen small spaces all over the country. Sure, there's the obvious small New York City apartment, but there's also the small beach bungalow house in Venice, California; the over-the-garage apartment in Miami; the dorm room in Virginia; the small hunting cabin in Texas. Small spaces are not restricted solely to urban areas, and my tips and ideas will translate effectively whether you're in an apartment or a house. In addition to giving you a gazillion ideas on how to help your little home work as efficiently as possible, this book is also chock-full of beautiful images that you can use to copy, mold, or inspire your own design. Occasionally in this book you'll see pictures of spaces that don't look super small, but I have included them because I think there may be something you can pull from them to use as a springboard for your own design style. I'm all about giving you as much

information as possible—think of this as the "full-service salon" of design books; you'll get loads of tips and ideas as well as great-looking spaces to pull from. You're going to give your home a little TLC, and it will love you for it!

In the past five years—first as the lead host/designer of FOX's makeover show *Design Invasion,* and now as a design expert on HGTV's *Small Space, Big Style* and as a regular contributor to *Decorating with Style* magazine—I have ventured into hundreds of homes across the country, finding solutions and offering inspirations for small spaces. I've tackled everything from reworking the layout for a tiny bedroom, to creating a new color scheme for a small living room, to making a closed-in kitchen appear larger. Working with real people in their real homes has inspired me to share what I've learned with other folks who want to live beautifully in smaller spaces. One of the most exciting elements in shooting a makeover show is the reaction or "reveal" when the homeowner walks in at the end of the day and sees the once-depressing, uninspired room transformed into an inviting, chic space (and it's always so cool when they burst into tears of joy). I realize I'm not solving all of the world's problems by decorating someone's home, but I honestly believe that when you love where you live, that joy manifests itself in all aspects of your life.

In my travels I have noticed that "small" is the new "big," often a preferred lifestyle for first-time home-owners, for growing families redefining their existing space, and for downsizing empty nesters. Small spaces are also a great choice for someone who's looking to live a "green" lifestyle; lots of folks want to leave a smaller carbon footprint on the planet, and smaller homes naturally require less energy and water. The ideas of reuse, repurpose, and recycle are a perfect fit for people living in a smaller space who want to be ecofriendly as well as cost conscious.

The small-space movement is so pervasive that I am designing a line of small-space furniture to fulfill the needs of small-space dwellers. I live in New York City, where space is precious—I know that I would like to have pieces that can serve more than one purpose, and so would all of my friends. When you have less space, you need to make the pieces you do have work hard and earn their keep; a chest of drawers also moonlights as a bedside table, your desk doubles as your dining table, and a tall bookshelf acts as your headboard. When you live in a box, you need to be crafty and clever and think *outside the box,* and I'm going to teach you how to do that!

In these last few years, people have stepped back and taken notice of how big things have grown—from cars to couches to cheeseburgers. We've been faced with the consequences of "living large," whether in the cost of filling up those cars, gaining weight, carrying hefty mortgages, or just living with *stuff* everywhere! So many of us want to simplify our lives, to get back to the basics, to what really matters—and of course that translates into the spaces we choose to live in, and how we live in them. Everyone I know feels like a million bucks after cleaning out a closet or decluttering a desk: Small spaces give you the feeling that you are in complete control—that your home isn't running you, you are running it. When things at home are manageable and contained, that contentment and clear-headed feeling is bound to carry over into other areas of your life.

But living with less doesn't mean living without luxury. People want style, elegance, and comfort, and they are realizing they can have that in any space. My specialty is in providing simple, smart solutions to small-space quandaries. I deliver practicality and inspiration at the right price point: It doesn't take a lot of money to achieve a warm and inviting atmosphere. And it doesn't always take an architect or a contractor to implement the changes you want. It takes motivation and some imagination—and a sense of humor! Design should be fun, not painful. Instead of giving you complicated, hard-to-follow recipes, I offer you "Cooking 101" for design. This book consists of tangible ideas that anyone can do easily.

Put This Book to Work for You and Your Space

I've come up with literally hundreds of tips—or decorating "tricks of the eye"—for solving common problems and making your space, whether it's 200 or 1,500 square feet, look and feel larger than it is. I've structured the book chapters around the following spaces: living rooms, dining rooms, kitchens, bathrooms, bedrooms, home offices, and hallways. Each of these chapters will include these features:

- **A series of common problems (frustrations!) and their solutions**
- **Libby's Tricks of the Trade—insider design tips and exact "how-to" instructions**
- **Lots of photos illustrating small-space design tips and ideas**

The book will also provide sample layouts and "Before" and "After" photographs of transformed spaces to show you how to easily solve the problems presented. I want to arm you with the information you need to create huge differences in style and ambience without spending tons of money.

Deciphering Your Design Dilemmas

Before you can implement my ideas, you have to identify any problems you have. As it turns out, that's not so easy! Most people look bewildered at their small space. They know they aren't happy with it, but they can't identify why. Understanding *why* it feels that way is the first, crucial step to changing your space. Otherwise you are apt to make changes that won't solve the problem (and might make it worse!).

Sometimes my clients say things like "I can't figure out why my dining room seems so cold and unfeeling," and then I look up and see a ceiling light fixture with exposed bulbs and know right away that it's creating the chilly sensation. I also know that a chandelier with shades, or two buffet lamps, would make it feel so much warmer and inviting. Maybe a room feels boring because it lacks color, or it seems cramped due to a bad layout. I know how to help you get to the root of the problem and how to fix it. Don't worry, this is going to be fun—you have me to help you now!

The ABCs of Interior Design

I rely on four building blocks of design to identify and then solve problems. They are: layout—understanding how to use your space and working with the furniture you own or can repurpose; the addition of color; the use of light; and organization/storage solutions that create more space. These building blocks lay the foundation for *visually* creating more space as well as *literally* creating it. You can find the solution to a problem in any one of these areas or in a combination of them.

The first chapter of the book will offer an overview of how these building blocks work. Then, for each space, I'll walk you step-by-step through the process of defining its problem(s) and finding solutions with these building blocks. You will learn how to make your bedroom, or your living room, or perhaps that corner you'd like to dine in look and feel more open. You will be able to create a space that is organized, gracious, and comfortable. And honestly, it will be easy, inexpensive, and fun!

Small Spaces, Big Mistakes!

These are the top ten mistakes people make in small spaces. I'm going to give you ideas, tips, and permission to break all the rules (you think you know) and turn your small space into the home you'll love! The biggest mistakes are:

1. Leaving your walls white. White walls won't technically make your space larger and they lack personality. Spice up your space, have a little fun and paint some color on your walls!

2. Using large-scale furniture. Oversized pieces can hog square footage but using better-proportioned furniture can allow you to create a more functional and comfortable living space.

3. Lack of light. Not lighting your space effectively makes it look smaller, if you can't see an area in your room it's as if it's not there! Capitalizing on natural light and bringing in artificial light is imperative.

4. Using short shelving and cabinetry. Using full-scale shelves and cabinets that go all the way up to the ceiling visually draw the eye upward making the ceiling seem higher and your space feel larger.

5. Keeping clutter. Holding onto too much stuff and not throwing away clutter can make even a large space feel small so, when in doubt, throw it out!

6. Using small-scale accessories. Large lamps, artwork, candles, vases, and accessories create the appearance of greater space and more height. No wimpy lamps!

7. Not using mirrors. Mirrors reflect light, whether it's daylight or lamplight, and they visually make your space feel larger by adding depth and dimension.

8. Not capitalizing on your wall space. Think vertically and get your walls working for you! Mount shelving or storage systems up on your walls to display collections and store items so you don't waste precious table space. This will also help focus your items in one spot so your space feels more organized.

9. Using all wood furniture. It makes a room feel clunky and bottom heavy, but by mixing in glass-topped tables with wood pieces you give your room a lighter, airier, and more open feel.

10. Using small area rugs. A small area rug can look like a postage stamp and make your room feel cramped but using a large rug creates an extended visual line and gives the illusion of more square footage.

{ Libby's Basic Toolbox }

Here's a breakdown of tools you should have in your design arsenal, and the cliché of "the right tool for the right job" is a cliché for a reason. You shouldn't use a butter knife to tighten a screw, scissors to cut wire, or your feet to measure square footage. Shortcuts like that can get you into big trouble in the design department. But never fear: Copy this list and take it with you to your local home improvement store, load up on the items you're missing, and I promise you'll be ready to tackle your project no matter how big or small it may be.

Keeping in mind that you most likely don't have some enormous garage in which to store tons of tools, I've included my essential list, which contains the basic items you'll absolutely need at some point in your adult life. They will all fit in a nice compact toolbox that won't take up loads of space. I've also given you some reasons *why* you need these tools as well as *how* to use them. I wish I could come to your place and help you with your project, but now it's up to you! Other than some imagination and inspiration, a tricked-out toolbox is the best place to begin your makeover!

- **Toolbox**: It may sound basic, but it feels good when you have a spot where you know you'll easily find everything you need. If you don't have room for a standard toolbox, get a long plastic storage box with wheels that is designed to fit under a bed. Put all of your tools in that and store it under your bed or sofa.

- **Cordless drill**: Spend a little extra for the cordless, because it gives you the freedom to move around without dragging an extension cord behind you. Get an extra battery and keep it charged so that you don't have to stop in the middle of a project to charge the battery.

- **Hammer**: You don't need an enormous, heavy hammer unless you're doing serious carpentry; a little smaller-scale, lighter-weight hammer is fine for hanging pictures and work along those lines.

- **Screwdriver**: Get an all-in-one model that allows you to store different tips in the handle; they switch out easily, and you don't have a million screwdrivers floating around in your kit.

- **Wire cutters**: I use these for everything—they are invaluable! Women should get a pair with a soft handle, which makes it easier to really grab onto them, squeeze hard, and cut something thick.

- **Adjustable wrench**: Again, you don't have to get the super-heavy-duty model unless you're doing serious carpentry. Buy a midsize model that will work for many jobs.

- **Glue gun**: Even the least crafty people still need a good old glue gun. Just make sure you buy the right size glue sticks for your model.

- **Staple gun**: If possible buy an electric staple gun; you can work much faster and easier than with a regular staple gun, and there's less wear and tear on your hand muscles and joints. This is an essential if you want to apply fabric to your walls and upholster a headboard or seat cushion. It's great for folks who don't see themselves as a hammer-and-nail–type person . . . it's just a staple gun, how scary can that be?

- **Tape measure**: An absolute must for measuring rooms, furniture, artwork . . . everything! Some models have extra-heavyweight tape that won't bend when you extend it out over a long span. Smaller versions include a little level in them, and they even make a battery-operated motorized tape measure.

- **Zip ties**: These are the secret weapons for most professional carpenters—they are little adjustable plastic ties that are superstrong and can hold just about anything. You know when you're doing something and you say, "I just need something to hold this together?" That's where zip ties come in; they are invaluable and can serve many purposes. For example, they are super at holding together that mess of cords under your desk.

- **Level**: This can be a small version of a level, only about 10 inches long. You really only need it to make sure pictures, shelves, and wall-mounted items are level and not crooked!

- **Extension cords**: I buy these in a bunch of different lengths and have them standing by. I like to plug them into the wall sockets in a room *before* I move in any furniture. That way, when you move in that armoire or sleeper sofa that weighs a ton, the cord is already plugged in behind it, and you don't have to move it a second time when you want to plug in lamps or electronics.

- **Awl**: This is a great tool for starting holes before you drill into a wall, but it also helps you poke holes in lots of things. You've probably never heard of it, but once you have one you'll be shocked by how much you use it!

- **Masking tape**: An oldie but a goodie, I use masking tape for framing pictures in mattes and so many other things I can't even count.

- **String/Twine**: A simple item that you'll eventually need at some point. You don't need to buy a colossal roll of it; a small roll will suffice.

- **Hardware**: Boxes of picture hangers, medium nails, panel nails, brads, mirror hangers, wall anchors/toggles with screws to fit, drywall screws; you'll most likely stock up on these items when you need something for a specific job, but it's handy to have some general hardware in your kit at the ready.

- **Pad of paper and pencil**: Pretty straightforward but nice to have in there so you can calculate measurements when hanging pictures and such.

- **Heavy-duty scissors**: You'll use these so much (opening that evil plastic packaging that you always cut your finger on), you'll be lucky if they actually stay in the tool kit!

Chapter One

THE NITTY-GRITTY OF DESIGN—

Layout, Color, Light, and Organization/Storage

The four building blocks of design that I referred to in the Introduction serve as useful tools for helping me uncover problem areas and find solutions to them. They can literally craft more space while also visually creating the illusion of more space. These are the four building blocks:

- **Layout:** understanding how to maximize your space and create multifunctional environments with the furniture you own (or can acquire)
- **Color:** knowing how to choose and use color to change the feel of your space and create your own personal style
- **Light:** creating ambience; how to get the most from your natural light and ways to brighten your space with artificial light
- **Organization/storage solutions:** finding storage space in places and in ways you would never have imagined

It can be difficult to step back and take an objective look at a space you've lived in for a while. Often you simply can't imagine it laid out any other way than it has been. Sometimes you know there's something missing or not functioning as well as it should, but you don't know where to begin to fix it! As a designer, when people come to me and say, "I don't like having people over to my place because I don't think it's very comfortable," with a little prodding I can usually figure out what's missing and how to fix the design. I ask my clients a number of questions, such as:

- How many lamps do you have?
- Are there overhead light fixtures?
- Where do you sit when you're in your room?
- What's your layout like?
- Are there any windows?
- What's on your floors?

It's almost like a he said/she said game; the client tells me one thing, and I read between the lines to determine what's really going on, half interior designer and half life coach. I think it's fun to try to decipher what people are *really* saying, find the root of their design problems, arm them with ideas to make changes, and then finally see how much they love their new design. Often these design dilemmas refer back in some way to layout, color, light, and organization. Now that you know these four building blocks of design, you can begin to rethink your own space and use the tips and tools in this book to envision your own small-space solutions.

Layout Lessons 101

Most people who want to redefine a small space—whether it's a room or an entire home—don't know where to begin. Whether they plan to use all new furniture or, even trickier, use existing pieces from a former (and perhaps larger) home, first and foremost they need to understand how to lay out their space. If they don't understand the proportions of their rooms and the ways to maximize those spaces, they cannot achieve the atmosphere they want and the functionality they need.

Layouts are as simple as measuring your room and all of your furniture, recording this information on a piece of paper, and moving the furniture around until you have the most effective positioning. Layouts give you the ability to look at your space as a whole, which allows you to craft a cohesive design plan rather than arranging your furnishings together piecemeal, which can feel like a hodgepodge of space that doesn't really work. Frequently people will say, "I need more storage," so they go out and buy a little chest of drawers. Then six months later they have to buy another little piece of furniture to hold everything. Well, they do that a few more times, and suddenly the space is full of tons of little storage pieces. Meanwhile, if they had done a layout, they may have been able to buy one large, functional piece that would make their space feel less cluttered, look better, and serve their storage needs more effectively.

The first thing I advise my clients to do is measure the entire space of the room. (All

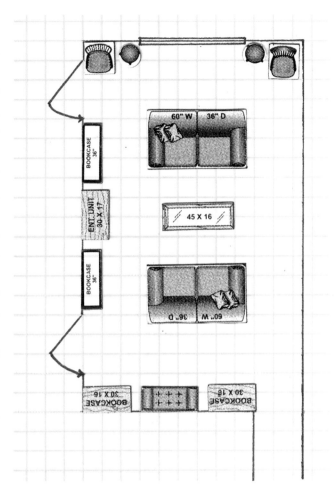

spaces are not created equal; for the play-by-play on exactly how to lay out your space, turn to page 40.) On a piece of graph paper, draw out the space's boundaries or perimeter. Often, when you look at a space on paper, both the problem and any number of creative solutions open up—ones you wouldn't have seen otherwise. For example, many people lay out their rooms with what I call the "wallflower theory." Remember those sixth grade school dances, held in a big gymnasium with a bunch of chairs pushed up against the four walls? It wasn't very conducive to making kids feel comfortable and not a real good use of the space either (poor kids). Well, the same holds true for your rooms: Don't assume that all the furniture has to be pushed up against a wall, because that usually leaves an enormous open area in the middle of the room. And unless you're a wrestler, we can probably come up with a better way to make use of that open area.

Designers often use the term *float* with regard to furniture, and this simply means to place pieces out into the middle of the room rather than up against a wall. Maybe a better use of the space would be to place your bookcase up against one wall but float your sofa out into the middle of the room facing the bookcase, and then place your desk up against the back of the sofa. A great way to gather ideas for cool layouts is to sort through photographs in home-design magazines; you may be inspired to completely reconfigure your existing pieces in a whole new way.

Layouts serve as springboards for ideas. Be bold and try new things, and if you don't like them, you can always put everything back the way it was originally! Another easy and effective way to help you visualize what you want from your space—and how to get it—is to look at room displays in department stores or in furniture brochures. In particular, seeing furniture in a real space helps you understand scale in a way that even pictures often can't illustrate.

Once you have your new layout, you need to measure your existing furniture to see if it will fit in the space you have allocated for it. Conversely, if you are buying something new, make sure it will fit in its designated space. Measure the *area* where that

piece is meant to go and then take your tape measure to the store and measure the piece you are buying. Be sure to measure the width of your front door as well as any hallways or elevators that the piece will need to pass through, and double-check that it can be moved through any turns or awkward spaces that you'd have to maneuver to get to your front door. Perhaps this advice sounds obvious, but size and scale are truly deceptive. Believe me: Costly mistakes occur all the time when people simply make assumptions. It's not unusual for someone to buy a sofa he or she likes, only to find that it won't fit through the living room door!

Here's a typical example of what happens: You decide you want to place your oversize armchair kitty-corner in your bedroom. But if you haven't measured the dimensions of both the chair and the space, you could easily find that the chair's width (*not* its depth) pushes the chair halfway out into the room and leaves virtually no walking space—not to mention the huge amount of wasted space it creates behind it! Using your tape measure and a piece of graph paper would have made the problem evident from the outset. And it could help you find another place in your home to use the chair.

Quality, Not Quantity: Defining Your Space with Multifunctional Furniture

In a small home every piece of furniture needs to serve more than one purpose. Too much furniture not only hogs the space but also makes it look even smaller than it is. In addition, people are creating

smaller living areas within their overall floor plans. Maybe you don't have a separate dining room, so you need to create an eating nook in your kitchen or a dining spot in your living room. Most small spaces don't have an office, so you may need to incorporate your desk into your bedroom or dining area. Or perhaps you live in a one-room studio that needs to function as living, dining, and sleeping area all in one!

You need furniture to help you delineate these spaces and break up the area so that one room can act as all rooms. And convertible furniture—items that can literally transform from one piece to the next (Clark Kent by day and Superman by night)—is even more of a necessity, because it helps divide the room and allows you to sit, stow, and store. The bottom line is that furniture in a small space needs to work harder for you than if it were in a large space.

Top left: You can push a dining table or tall pub table up against a wall and use one side for seating. When you entertain, pull it off the wall and use all four sides—this is a great use of the entryway.

Top right: This bar not only helps divide the living and dining spaces but it doubles as a bookshelf and display unit for colorful accessories; you want to use storage any way you can get it!

A window seat is a great way to maximize seating as well as create extra storage underneath.

Happy Hues— Add a Little Color

I can't even begin to tell you how important color is to any space. It's a soapbox moment for me when I start talking about the virtues of color, but I have literally seen it transform everything from walls, to furniture, to someone's mood! There's color therapy for a reason: It helps create a feeling and sets the overall tone in a home. There are so many ways that you can incorporate color into your small space and have some fun, as well as express your personality. Whether you select a rich, bold, exciting color or a soft, pale, relaxing hue, you'll soon learn to accept color as your companion.

Perk Up Your Place with Paint

Using a few cans of paint is definitely the quickest, least expensive way to transform a room. If you buy neutral furniture (tan, black, white, or gray), you can easily change your wall color for an entirely new feel without having to go out and purchase new furniture (which costs much more than a few cans of paint!). Colored furniture, such as a red, blue, or green sofa, limits the changes you can make; they may be subtler and less gratifying than freshly painted walls. I'm always fascinated when people buy a green sofa but are petrified to use green paint on their walls. They put all the pressure on their furniture to inject color and make their space feel inviting, but by leaving their walls white they are fighting an uphill battle. Here's the bottom line: You'll get more impact and make less of a commitment or financial investment if you apply color to your walls.

Yet "paint fear" truly is an epidemic, and not only for the small-space dweller. Walk into any paint store and watch the sea of people standing there, looking incredibly confused and undecided. Sifting through a color wheel is not especially comforting. Moreover, people overwhelmingly believe that leaving their walls white makes their space look larger. It doesn't. White walls effectively convey one thing: You are living in a boring, small white space! Darker colors not only add life to a room, but used carefully can make the walls of a small room recede. So once we have laid out a room, I help my clients feel comfortable experimenting with colors—often very bold ones—effectively.

At first, using strong colors takes a leap of faith, since the application of color works differently in every room. Paint changes the feeling of a space through its richness and hues. Because these qualities shift with available light and the shadows it creates, working with paint takes time and a willingness to take some chances. I wouldn't suggest that someone paint four walls in

These wide stripes take a small room with a low ceiling and visually make it look larger; the colors are still pale enough so that it doesn't look like a circus. The trundle bed is a great place to store seasonal items below (instead of having a mattress in the trundle drawer).

Top left: If you don't love your brick, whether it's painted or natural, don't be afraid to paint it. Here the homeowners wanted a Tuscan look, so I painted the white brick they already had with three different paint color layers to add some warmth to the room.

Top right: I used a small sponge roller and added the next layers with a rag—it was incredibly easy and made a huge difference in the overall look and feel of the room!

dark eggplant, but I do encourage people to think outside the box, shed their fears, and have a little fun. If they don't like the result, it's just paint—and in a small space, painting doesn't take much time or money to redo!

Clearly color appearances change from day to night, so be sure to look at how the color you're considering looks at different times of day. It's also helpful to think about when you're actually in your space most. If you're away in an office all day, primarily consider how the paint looks at night; if you work from home in your small space, observe how the color appears during the day.

If you're not sure where to begin with color, pick up some home magazines that showcase the style you're after and flip through until you find a wall color you like. Nine times out of ten, the magazine will list the exact paint color. If it doesn't, you can at least tear out the page and bring it with you to your local hardware or paint store, where someone may be able to suggest similar

colors. When you find the right paint chip, bring it home and tape it to your wall for a while or look at it against your furniture or fabrics in the room you plan to paint. Some retailers are even creating opportunities to help customers match paint to their decor. Pottery Barn, for instance, has created a paint partnership program with Benjamin Moore that gives the consumer the exact shades they use in their catalogues and retail stores. This service eliminates the fear and guesswork for the consumer, encouraging him or her to take some chances (and undoubtedly racks up more sales for the store). Everyone benefits.

Another wonderful characteristic about paint is that it makes items you already have look completely different. Paint brings out the detail in your woodwork, artwork, and all of your furnishings. It helps you rethink what you already have . . . and that's a great place to begin when you're watching what you spend.

Left: Here's the brick wall that started out white. After I finished painting it over with three different tan colors the wall added depth and dimension to the space.

Far left: This white mirror really pops on a chocolate brown wall—if it were on a white wall, you'd barely notice it!

Left: Don't be afraid to have some fun with a bright color. Remember, it's just paint—when you are tired of it, you can easily paint a new color!

If you have old hand-me-down furniture from college or a first apartment, get some more mileage out of it by painting it. It will save you money short term but you can still make over your space and achieve the design you want!

Insta-Room!: Get All New Furniture with a Can of Paint

You know that hand-me-down wall unit from your parents or that coffee table you found at a yard sale—it's some sort of weird gold oak color that you hate, but you can't afford or don't have the time to get something new? I'm giving you permission to PAINT IT! If you don't love it as it is, go ahead and give it an inexpensive face-lift. Now I'm not recommending you do this to the table you received as a family heirloom from your grandmother, but for furniture that's not super sentimental or valuable, I say go for it!

If you have loads of mismatched pieces of furniture, you can update the look and create a cohesive design by painting them all the same color. The old way of thinking would have required you to spend lots of time sanding the wood before you actually painted it, but now there's a gel solution called Liquid Sandpaper that you simply rub on the wood, let sit for thirty minutes, wipe off, and your surface is ready to paint. This works on kitchen cabinets, bed frames, shelving units, tables, and most any case goods (see Libby's Glossary of Design Terms on page 158). Basically, you can paint wood furniture but not upholstery . . . pull the trigger and paint an old end table, but don't spray paint your sofa.

When painting wood furniture use the same water-based latex paint that you'd use for your walls. Apply the paint onto the surface with a roller and then spread the paint with a brush; this will speed up the process and give you more even coverage. You can achieve various design styles depending on the paint color you choose to use:

- **Contemporary/Sleek**: Use black paint in a high-gloss or semigloss finish.

- **Shabby chic/Beachy**: Use white paint in a satin or semigloss finish.

- **Cool modern hotel**: Use dark black/brown paint in a high-gloss finish.

- **Classic country**: Use white paint in an eggshell finish, and after painting gently rub sandpaper on some of the corners and edges to show the wood below for the classic country distressed effect.

You'll be surprised the way you can transform your room by not only updating the color on your walls but the color on your furniture!

Here's the same wall unit, but we just painted it black. It completely transformed the look of that tired old oak furniture to a hip, cool piece that looks pulled together and fresh!

{Painting 101}

Okay, I know I keep encouraging you to get some color up on your walls, so I'm going to give you some quick tips on how to paint like a pro! The worst part of painting is moving your stuff (at least it inspires you to clear out the clutter) and the prep work before the first brush stroke ever hits the wall. That said, preparing ahead of time not only allows you to work quickly and saves you time in the long run, but when you return everything to its place, you truly have cleared things out, which gives you a sense of order and organization. Don't be overwhelmed by all the details here . . . it's much easier to paint than it sounds; I just want to give you the blow-by-blow if you've never done it before. I'm one of those wacky people who actually enjoys painting; I put on some great music and get to work. You never know: You might find it to be therapeutic!

If you're still really nervous about the painting process, consider hosting what I call a "painting party." Invite a bunch of close friends to come over in casual painting attire; you supply the brushes, paint, and supplies as well as some good music, pizzas and beer, or Mexican food and margaritas. Be sure to send thank you notes the next day, as these people are truly excellent friends!

Laying the Groundwork: Prepping to Paint

· Move out the furniture or push it to the middle of the room and cover it.

· Cover the floors with drop cloths or plastic tarps. (I like cotton drop cloths or old sheets, because sometimes the plastic ones can be a little slippery.)

· Using 2-inch-wide blue painter's tape, mask all the baseboards, crown molding, and door trim. If you plan to paint your trim first, then mask off the wall, ceiling, and floor areas.

· Remove switch plates, picture hooks, and nails. If you know that some artwork or mirrors are going right back where they were, leave those hooks and nails in the wall! Fill any holes with a bit of joint compound, let it dry, and sand it.

· Prime unfinished wood and semigloss or glossy walls. Some new paint formulations don't require priming, but they can be more expensive. If it lets you skip painting an additional coat, however, you may think it's worth it!

· Create a staging area where you keep all supplies, paints, brushes, pans, rollers, and rags, and make sure there's a drop cloth under everything!

Items to Buy

· **Rollers and sleeves:** Buy standard size and a $\frac{3}{8}$-inch nap roller. This will cover most wall surfaces from smooth to semirough. If your walls have much more texture, use a $\frac{1}{2}$-inch nap roller; it will give you better coverage. Buy lots of extra roller sleeves, because you'll want to have them to switch out when it's time to change colors. They are not really washable when you move from room to room and need to paint a new color.

· **Banana roller:** This is a smaller version of the standard roller and is super helpful in small areas where a standard roller would be too big. It fits in tight spots, plus I just like the name of it!

- **Paintbrushes:** Get two sizes, a $3\frac{1}{2}$" inch and a 2 inch. Get nylon bristle brushes and make sure they are angled—this will help you paint a finer line when you cut edges near moldings and trim.
- **Drop cloths, rags, paint trays, and tray liners**
- **Stepladder:** If you have high ceilings (lucky you!), get a small version of a standard ladder.
- **Blue painter's tape:** Get a few rolls of the 2-inch size.
- **Small tub of joint compound** or spackle and 220-grit sandpaper
- **Paint!**

Get Your Color On: How to Begin

- If you have crown molding, baseboard, and door trim that needs painting, then paint that first. Mask off the wall areas surrounding it with painter's tape and use semigloss paint. In my opinion a fresh white color always looks the freshest and best on trim.

- When it comes to painting your walls, you'll want to cut all the edges first (where you've masked the blue tape over the trim) using the $3\frac{1}{2}$-inch brush. Cutting refers to using a brush to paint the area of a wall that is next to the ceiling, baseboard, or door/window trim; it allows you to apply the paint more precisely in a tighter area than a roller does. Don't be shy about how much paint you have on your brush; you don't want it dripping, but the brush shouldn't be dry or you won't get enough coverage on the wall. Start by adding color in the corner next to the tape with the angled part of the brush, and then paint a thicker line by flattening the brush up against the wall. This line will equal the width of the brush, which will give you enough of a cushion to roll into once you begin rolling.

- Now that you've cut a border of paint around the wall with your brush, it's time to fill in with the roller. This is the fun part, because it goes so much faster and you really start to see the color come to life on your wall! Fill a paint tray with paint, dip the roller in, and roll it around in the tray a few times to completely cover it with paint. Roll the paint from the top down; roll it up into the $3\frac{1}{2}$"-inch

I love painting!

paintbrush line you already cut at the ceiling and then down to the paintbrush line at the baseboard. If you can roll all the way up and all the way down in one motion, it gives you more even coverage. Make sure to keep the roller wet but not dripping—if the roller is too dry and there's not enough paint, it will be sheer and definitely take three coats.

- If you can't finish the job in one day, you can preserve the roller and paintbrush overnight by getting them wet with paint and then completely wrapping them in plastic wrap. They will be airtight, and when it's time to begin the next day, you can simply unwrap them and get back to work.

- Save leftover paint in clear glass jars, seal them tightly, and label them with the room the color was used in. If you need to touch up the paint at some point, you will have easy access to the paint and know exactly what color goes where.

- One last thing I recommend is not to judge your paint color until you've removed all the blue painter's tape. Some people have trouble envisioning what the final outcome will look like, and that blue tape certainly doesn't help! Once you remove the tape and artfully place your belongings back into the room and hang your pictures on the walls, then, and only then, are you allowed to judge your color!

Wallpaper Wonderland

Wallpaper has made a huge comeback. Right now there are all types of trendy and traditional patterns in a wide range of color schemes—from soft and subtle to bold and bright—that are sure to perk up any room. Textured papers such as silk, sea grass, and embossed vinyl are popular as well. Unfortunately, the "fear of commitment" about applying something to your wall that's not so easy to remove reigns supreme. And the cost of wallpaper is often prohibitive. Plus, if you are renting or subletting a space, it's not practical. But I have a few ideas for how to incorporate all the fun and fabulousness of your favorite wallpaper without actually applying it to your walls:

- **Table toppers** Cut a piece (or pieces) of wallpaper the size of your coffee table (this also works great on an end table or kitchen table) and then have a piece of glass cut to the size of the table as well (just about any hardware store can order it for you). Lay the glass on the table over the wallpaper and you now have a great view of your favorite wallpaper. Sea grass or textured fabric wallpapers are perfect for this, and it's a great way to update an old table as well!

- **Instant headboard** Buy three large poster frames and frame your favorite wallpaper pattern in them. Hang all three on the wall behind your bed, and you'll have an inexpensive and dramatic headboard. This also works well with different patterns in each frame, but make sure the patterns use the same color schemes or it will look like a circus!

- **Chic shelving** You can pack a punch with a great wallpaper by papering just the inside back section of a shelving unit; it's quick and easy to do, and you achieve the look you want without it taking over your entire room.

- **Screen gem** Cover a folding screen with your favorite wallpaper print; you can staple it on with a staple gun and then hot glue ribbon trim over the edges to cover the staples. You can place it in a corner of your room as a focal point, or you can place it behind a sofa or your bed to create an accent wall. Or, if you live in a really small space, such as a city studio, you can use it to divide your living area, such as separating where you sleep from your "living room."

- **Closet case** Wallpaper the inside of your closet and the insides of your closet doors; it can be subtle and elegant or wild and crazy. It's a blast of unexpected color and pattern, and it's guaranteed to make you smile even on a rainy Monday morning!

Wallpaper gave this old table some new life; it's a simple, low-commitment way to add a little zip to your space!

Left: By wallpapering just the back insides of the shelves, you get to enjoy the fun look of wallpaper without having it take over an entire wall.

Below: An even lower-commitment way to enjoy wallpaper would be to just tack it in with thumbtacks on the edges and in the corners of the shelves rather than gluing it.

Once you get the wallpaper up, don't fill up your shelves so full that you don't get to appreciate the pattern (I know you're tired of hearing this but throw some stuff out!).

- **Wallpaper albums** Buy twelve to sixteen square record album frames and frame wallpaper in each one. Hang them on the wall together as a group, leaving 2 inches in between each one. You can hang any configuration you like, just make sure there's an even 2 inches around each one. It's a perfect way to get wallpaper on your walls without the impending doom of having to remove it one day!

- **Made in the shade** This is an "oldie but goody." Cover a drum lampshade with your favorite wallpaper and hot glue a thin ribbon on the upper and lower edges for a little extra zip. Just remember two's the limit; any more wallpaper lampshades than that and you'll visually clutter up your room.

It Was A Total Fabrication!

Fabric on walls can soften the overall feel of small spaces, and in a small bedroom it cre- ates the feel of an intimate haven—perfect and peaceful. Fabric helps baffle sound if you live in a noisy apartment, and it's easy to apply to your walls using a staple gun. Once it's mounted, cover the staples with ribbon or any trim of your choice, using hot glue. Or, if you want to use fabric on a really small wall, such as one between two beams, you can even use a heavy curtain and hang it with tension rods between the two beams. Unlike wallpaper, fabric can be easily removed when you want a change!

Pump Up The Color Volume With Accents

Punches of color perk up your space and give it personality. You can add a hit of color anywhere in a room in a number of ways. I like to think of accents as "low-commitment color"—you can achieve a big impression with a quick color hit. Plus you can easily change these accents when you want a fresh look.

Libby's before and afters:

Before: You want to think about color on your walls rather than putting the pressure on your furniture to bring in all the color. By keeping most of your furniture neutral, you're allowed to easily and inexpensively change the color scheme of the room by changing paint and accessories.

After: There's a bold wall color and a neutral sofa, but I broke up the dark wall by hanging some drapery panels floor to ceiling behind the sofa; it creates an accent wall and adds some great color and softness. Going all the way up to the ceiling with the drapes visually draws your eye upward and makes the ceiling seem higher and the room feel larger.

{Libby's Low-Commitment Color Hits}

Inject some fun into your space with bright accessories; they are easy enough to replace when you want a new color scheme.

Sometimes just one brightly colored object can add an entirely new design element to your space; a little can go a long way.

Throw blankets are a great way to spice up your room and add a comfy factor as well.

Fresh flowers are a quick way to add a little zip to your room— treat yourself! You deserve it!

- Vases
- Throw blanket
- Throw pillows
- Small ottomans
- Candlesticks
- Plates
- Shower curtain/towels
- Drapes
- Picture frames
- Small planters
- Bedding/dust skirt

Painting certain walls or pieces of furniture, such as end tables or the back of shelving units, can be extremely effective. You can easily create accents with fabrics—headboards, pillows, bedspreads, area rugs—and with wallpaper.

Think about contrast when looking at what color to paint a wall that has artwork on it; if your artwork is light, paint the wall dark, and if the artwork is dark, paint the wall light. You really want it to pop off the wall! You also want to use large artwork when using a bold wall color; large artwork also makes a small room feel bigger.

You can enjoy a great hit of color by painting just the inside back section of a wall unit; here the navy blue adds depth and dimension.

This white frame looks great on the green wall— if the wall were white, it might look a little blah.

In both small and large spaces, I consistently notice the use of certain colors as accents: chocolate brown, caramel, aqua, bright orange, citron green, and icy gray blue. See Libby's Greatest Color Hits, featured on page 154 of the book, to see my favorite/recommended color combinations.

I encourage people to paint one accent wall in a room a bold color and paint the other three walls a neutral tan. A tan color helps balance the bolder-colored wall while adding more life than simple white or off-white walls can—it looks more deliberate and conscious. This adds some punch and a hit of color without closing in your space. Traditionally, good candidates for accent walls are those with a fireplace, a bed, or a sofa. You want to make that wall the visual focus of the room.

If you really don't love color, consider painting all four walls a neutral tan. Tan has more zip to it than white or off-white. It also creates good contrast, making artwork and furniture really pop. Tan also adds more dimension than white or off-white, but it remains neutral enough to mix well with all colors. If you are truly terrified to use color, go ahead and leave your walls white and light (although I'm secretly encouraging you to put even the palest color on your wall to add some personality to your space). You can easily change the look of your room in a matter of minutes by adding colored accessories, artwork, and china.

This may surprise you, but the most commonly used accessory in small spaces is artwork; it adds life and style to a room without using up valuable square footage. It may seem counterintuitive, but big visuals actually work well on walls in a small space. They add height, scale, and dimension. As an example, think of the long, narrow galley kitchens found in many apartments. If there is no window, hanging an oversize print on the far wall will distract from the narrow dimensions, making the kitchen feel much larger. Also, keep in mind that one lonely picture on a wall can call attention to the lacking square footage of your room. So hang large and small pieces together to create a grouping, or choose oversize artwork.

Finally, think in terms of 3s: An important part of what interior designers do to create an overall look has to do with the "styling" aspect of the space. They take accessories, simple or ornate, and artfully arrange them on shelving, mantles, and tabletops to achieve a "homey" lived-in look. This final stage takes a space from ordinary to extraordinary!

Two isn't enough.

Four feels like too much.

But three looks and feels just right!

Some people think in symmetrical terms, and if they have a vase on one end of the shelf, they feel they have to have another vase on the other end. This type of styling can give a room a robotic feel. Instead, consider balancing the vase with a stack of books, some candlesticks, or a green plant. (Turn to page 75 to see step-by-step instructions for exactly how to arrange a wall unit.)

The trick to arranging items like a pro is to think in terms of threes—two vases on a shelf are too little, four vases are too many, but three vases are just right! Also, mixing three objects in varying heights balances the scale and looks chic. Items can range from pillar candles to vases to books; these objects will help make your space look more like a home. Just don't go overboard, because you don't want it to look cluttered; a little styling goes a long way!

My mom is a designer and she taught me that objects and accessories look better arranged in threes ... always listen to your mother!

Let There Be Light

Lighting is critical to small spaces, because it has the power to make a room feel brighter and therefore much larger. Light changes the entire atmosphere of your home and makes it warm and inviting. By using various sources of light, you create layers in a room, resulting in a richer ambience. Given the trend toward dividing up small spaces, good lighting becomes even more essential. Closets serve as home offices; partitions separate living space from bedrooms. These are potentially gloomy digs if you don't know how to brighten them up.

The key to utilizing light lies in understanding the different ways to allow it to enter a room, create it when necessary, and not lose it. There are two kinds of light to work with—natural and artificial. The more natural light you can bring into a room, the better. Be careful not to obstruct views or natural light from windows and doors with furniture; use lower pieces such as benches, stools, and ottomans to keep the space open and capitalize on the good light you do have. For window treatments, translucent shades or sheers work better than blackout or opaque. They will eliminate the glare while maintaining a sense of openness. For additional light, be sure to use glass for room dividers. Screens with frosted glass, or shelving units with backs in frosted glass, allow for privacy while still allowing in plenty of natural light.

Artificial light can be tricky, and using it effectively changes from room to room. But dark square footage in a small space is like not having that square footage at all. If you can't see it, you don't get credit for it, so light it up! That said, you don't have to live with overhead lighting. It's depressing and colors the mood of a space. Remember: Light should be inviting and create a feeling of warmth, which you can never achieve from an overhead

Top left: Sheers are a great way to have some privacy but still let in valuable natural light.

Top right: Glass blocks let in natural light and can add an interesting design element to your space.

Top left: This fluorescent light box on the ceiling offered cold, harsh light and made the kitchen feel smaller because of the way it dropped down into the room. The dark wallpaper on the ceiling made it feel crowded and closed in.

Top right: By replacing the light box with simple drop-down pendants, recessed ceiling cans, and under-the-cabinet lighting, we added layers of light that make the room feel warmer and seem larger. Just paint and lighting were updated; we didn't change the kitchen cabinets, but see how different they look!

fluorescent bulb. You don't want to feel as if you're in a petri dish! If you have to use overhead lights, install a dimmer switch. Instead of overhead lighting, there are quite a few different types of artificial light you can try.

Lamp of Approval

Since you have less space, you want to avoid having any of it lost in darkness. Even in a small area, you can use as many as four or five lamps; this will ensure that light reaches even the corners of your room. People think that a small space calls for small lamps, but the opposite is true—large lamps add height and scale to a small room, making it feel larger.

No small, wimpy lamps—just good tall ones!

On the Right Track

When you have limited electrical and/or structural options, track lights offer a wonderful and relatively inexpensive solution. Any home improvement store will have them. In a dark kitchen, or one with no overhead ceiling fixture, you can mount track lighting with minimal fuss. You can control where track lights shine—angled on artwork, in dark corners, and so on. You can also clip individual lights onto the track however you wish to space them, adding to its versatility. If you are living temporarily in a space, some track-lighting kits enable you to mount the lights with adhesive tape and plug them into a nearby wall socket, as opposed to having to hire an electrician to hard wire them.

Picture Perfect

When you illuminate a dark spot, you feel as if you gain square footage. Picture lights can add depth to a space and add a wonderful glow when shining on artwork. But don't feel as if only expensive artwork warrants picture lights. They work just as well when placed over a large framed poster. You can also mount picture lights on top of shelving units to add drama and to illuminate the items in the unit.

The Great Recession

Recessed lights are metal cans literally recessed into your ceiling so that the can rests flush with the ceiling and doesn't drop down into your room at all. They come in

The different types of light in this kitchen—under cabinet, over cabinet, and recessed ceiling cans—illuminate the entire area, and when you can see the whole space, it feels bigger. You're not losing square footage to the dark.

Above left: It's great
to place a lamp
directly in front of
a mirror; when you
turn it on, it maxi-
mizes the amount of
light given off and
creates a nice glow.

Above right: If you
have smaller mirrors,
hang them on the
wall together in a
grouping; you'll
mimic the impact
of a single, larger
mirror.

many different sizes and take several different types of bulbs. They work especially
well in kitchens and hallways.

**Recessed lights function well in a small
room because they take up no area space and
don't bisect the room visually the way a chandelier does.** Just be sure to place them on a
dimmer, so that you can control the amount
of light. For instance, during the day you'll
want task light, but at night, for a dinner party, you may want to lower the lights
and add candles to enhance the ambience.
Recessed lights are also available with bulbs
that can be pointed or angled to illuminate
a certain area such as artwork on a wall or a
bookshelf. These are called wall washers and
can give the cool effect of an art gallery.

Under-Cabinet Lighting

**When possible, mounting lights beneath a wall
cabinet and above a countertop will provide
depth and dimension to a small space as well
as add light to your countertop work surface.**
In a kitchen or a work space, this kind of
lighting makes the room feel larger because
it literally adds another layer of available
light. Under-cabinet-lighting kits, as with
track-lighting kits, are available in most
home improvement stores.

Mirror, Mirror on the Wall

**Mirrors have been used for ages, because they
add natural light during the day and reflect
candlelight at night.** They also extend a
room, making it feel more open. To maximize a mirror's impact, you can position a
large mirror (don't worry if you have a tiny
room . . . a substantial mirror will make
it look so much bigger) on a wall directly
opposite a window or a glass door. It's like
adding another entire window, because the
reflection doubles the light and visually

opens up your space. Mirrored screens, large hanging mirrors, mirrored furniture, or shelving units/curios/armoires with the backs of the shelves covered in mirror are all home runs in a small space.

Savvy and Stylish Storage Solutions

The best way to create more physical space—besides putting an addition onto your home—is to create more storage. Storage lies at the heart of small-space functionality. By finding places for storing your belongings, you get them off the floor, tabletops, desktops, and countertops, and that adds square footage. With storage you also get the peace of mind knowing that everything's in its place and you'll be able to find what you need without sending out a search party. Most people can't afford

custom builders, but they still don't want to have to look at tons of stuff scattered all over their small space.

I have two steps to help create storage. First, assess the space in consideration: What do you need to store? For instance, in a bedroom you might need linen storage and in a kitchen more space for pots and pans. Pinpointing what you need the space for will help you find the space. Second, utilize multifunctional furniture or find new uses for old pieces. For example, in a bathroom, use a metal magazine rack to store rolled up towels and add pockets to the outside of your shower curtain to store hair accessories or toiletries.

Here are some smart storage solutions for everything imaginable—in any room in your home—to help you stay organized:

- If you're lucky enough to have a walk-in closet, cover one wall from floor to

Above left: Position a large mirror on a wall opposite a window; it will reflect natural light, brighten the room, and make your space look much larger.

Above right: Use large mirrors in small spaces; they trick the eye and open up your space.

ceiling with slat board or pegboard. You can use pegs and hooks to hold everything from purses, ties, belts, and necklaces. You can also hang a shower caddy on the slat board to hold items like perfumes and cologne.

- In a closet, use clear storage boxes if possible; they will save you tons of time by taking the guesswork out of exactly what is where.

- Repurpose wall-mount plate racks to hold files, magazines, and mail. They are shallow but tall and can hold a lot!

- Stack lots of plastic crates on top of each other and side-by-side to create a quick, inexpensive wall of storage. They come in tons of different colors, so you can have some fun with them. You can also use old wooden wine crates for an earthier look.

- Use a paper towel holder to hold ribbon and twine neatly in one spot.

- Mount a wire baking rack on the wall to display note cards (drape the cards over the wires) and clip photos and reminders to the wires with binder clips.

- Paint a bunch of cans of different sizes all the same color (high-gloss chocolate brown would be cool) and poke a hole in the back of each can with an awl (see Libby's Basic Toolbox on page xiv to learn about awls). Pull a little wire through each hole and attach a small metal-rimmed round tag to each can. You can use the tags to write the contents of each can. Screw cup hooks into the wall in a row and hang the cans from the ring of the metal-rimmed tag. Fill each can with whatever supply you need to have standing by at all times: In the office you'd have a can for pens, one for pencils, one for markers, and one for small Post-it pads; in the bathroom you'd have cans filled with Q-Tips, cotton balls, combs and hairbrushes, and toothbrushes and toothpaste; and in the kitchen you'd fill cans with to-go menus, small utensils, matchbooks, and cutlery.

- Replace the address section of a luggage tag with a label indicating what items are stored in nontransparent boxes and baskets.

- Mount metal hooks on a closet wall or inside a pantry door to hold basic hand tools like wire cutters and heavy-duty scissors.

- Wire baskets work well in every area of your small space, plus they are cheap and require no installation. There are versions that you set on top of your shelf to allow you to take advantage of vertical space, and there are under-shelf basket racks that you simply slide onto a shelf and the storage area you gain is below the shelf. Suddenly you have another whole shelf below your existing shelf! In the kitchen pantry they eke out a little extra space to store placemats or dish towels; in the bathroom they can hold hair dryers and small electronics; and in the office they can hold files that you need to access regularly.

- In a closet, under your sink, or on any shelving unit, you can place a shoe riser on an existing shelf to create another level of storage. Every inch counts, and if you have a 16-inch area

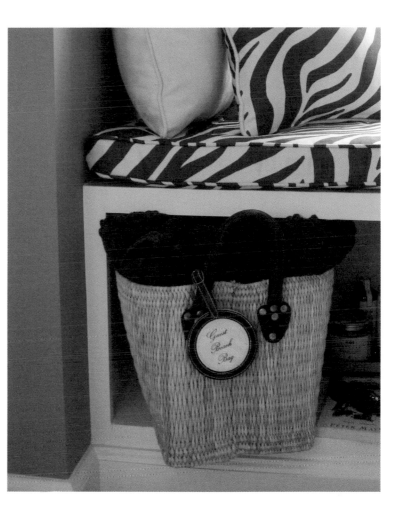

in between shelves but your items in that space are only 6 inches high, why not place something in between that allows you to double up and capitalize on the entire space?

- Use open shower curtain rings to suspend kitchen items like pot holders, dish towels, and measuring tools.

- A swivel wall rack (the ones you usually use in your closet to hang lots of pants on) can be used in many other areas of your small space. In your kitchen you can hang everything from dish towels and pot holders to utensils on S hooks; mounted up high on a hallway wall they can hold jackets, purses, and

Luggage tags can be a fun, attractive way to label stored items; they work on baskets, bins, and bags.

Top left: A simple wire shelf allows you to capitalize on the upper square footage area of a cabinet.

Top right: These S hooks come in several sizes and can be used in a myriad of ways to hold tons of different items!

tote bags; and in a bathroom they can hold towels, a hair dryer if it has a rubber hang loop, and a pouch filled with brushes and combs.

- Corner wire shelves typically used in showers can work in many different areas. They are super when used in a corner of the home office to eke out another space to stash files and office supplies. They also work well in an unused corner spot in the kitchen; they can hold cookbooks and regularly used oils, vinegars, and spices.

- Thread rolls of utility tape (masking, duct, and painter's tape), as well as

ribbon and twine, on a wooden suit hanger and hang them on the back of a hallway door for easy access.

- Create an all-in-one craft/wrapping station by placing a tool apron around a five-gallon bucket (the big white plastic ones that joint compound comes in). Place all the rolls of wrapping paper inside the bucket, and in the pockets of the apron place scissors, tape, tissue paper, ribbons, bows, markers, and gift cards.

Now that you have an understanding of design basics, it's time to tackle your problems, room by room!

LIBBY'S TRICKS OF THE TRADE

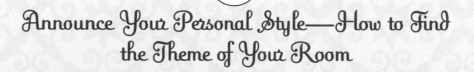

Announce Your Personal Style—How to Find the Theme of Your Room

I knew the client wanted a Moroccan design for her living room. The artwork hanging behind the sofa is actually a grass roller window shade from a home improvement store that I spray painted a Moorish design onto (I made a large stencil and just repeated it three times).

Often people will ask me how I come up with designs and themes for a person's room. I think they ask because they do not know where to begin formulating their own designs, and it can be overwhelming when you're starting from scratch.

I begin by looking at the person whose home I'm designing; I ask about their hobbies, interests, and favorite colors and use their answers as my springboard. If someone loves the beach, then I know they'll be happy in a room with colors in the following shades: tans, sand, soft

blue, creams, and pale aqua. If someone wants an Asian theme, they'll love colors of red, black, cream, and gold.

It's funny how people will leave me hints about what they really want their space to look like. I went into one woman's home and she had a floral chintz sofa and soft pale colors on all the walls and the other pieces of furniture. But hanging on the wall all by itself was the most beautiful Moroccan platter with dark rich colors in eggplant, gold, pink, and turquoise. Because she'd hung it in such an important place, I knew that she wanted a room with a Moroccan feel. I used the platter as the inspiration for my design, and it's a room she really adores! You can use all sorts of things as inspiration for the design of your space: a necklace, a favorite shirt or piece of clothing, a memorable vacation, a cherished movie, a cool hotel room . . . the possibilities are endless! If you still need a little help getting started, I've used the following design themes and colors in the past:

Big city: gray, cream, black, silver
• Paint one wall a rich dark gray. Use light cream upholstered furniture, black tables, steel and silver accent pieces, and lots of black-and-white photographs.

Country: yellow, brown, green, coral
• Paint the walls yellow, use a sage green for the upholstered pieces, mix in some patterned drapes and accessories, and use brown-stained wood tables and woodwork. Frame some silk scarves and hang them on the walls.

Tuscan/Italian: rust, black, tan, cream
• Paint the walls a rich rust/russet color. Use black accessories and natural-stained woodwork and keep it light with soft creams on the furniture and floor. Hang beautiful Italian platters and earthenware on the walls.

Hip hotel: black, tan, chocolate brown, gray, silver, cream
• Paint one wall a rich brown. Bring in tan and cream furniture and use high-gloss finishes, glass and silver/chrome accents on tables, and lots of black-and-white photographs in black frames.

Beach: tans, creams, caramel, pale blue, aqua
- Use beachy colors in any combination; tan or soft blue on the walls, whitewashed furniture and woodwork, crisp blue and white upholstery. Accessorize with seashells and coral. Frame ocean maps in white frames for wall décor.

Green: lime green, tan, chocolate brown, cream
- Use colors found in nature like tans, earthy browns, and bright greens and incorporate textures such as seagrass, bamboo, and rattan. Frame modern silk fern fronds and palm leaves in rich wood frames with white mats to bring in that botanical feel. Also add lots of plants.

Asian: red, black, gold, cream

- Paint one wall red and the other walls a soft tan. Use light cream–colored upholstered furniture and black wood accent tables and ottomans. Consider mounting an Asian screen on the wall as artwork.

Moroccan: eggplant, gold, hot pink, turquoise, chocolate brown

- Paint one wall a rich dark eggplant and paint the other walls a soft golden tan. Use tan upholstered furniture, bright pink and turquoise accents and accessories, and dark-stained wood pieces.

Shabby chic: pale blue, soft rose, white, silver

- Keep the walls bright white and bring in lots of white-painted furniture. Use a soft cotton patterned fabric on the upholstered pieces and white and silver accessories. Frame family pictures in silver frames.

Southwest: tans, turquoise, terra-cotta, cream

- Paint the walls a soft tan. Use cream upholstered furniture, turquoise and terra-cotta accents, and rich-stained wood pieces. Consider hanging a brightly colored southwestern rug on the wall.

African: tans, cream, brown, black
- Paint the walls tan. Use cream or earthy-colored upholstery, animal-patterned fabrics for pillows, and small items like ottomans; use dark-stained wood and hang sepia-toned pictures in groupings on the wall or frame pages from a photo book on Africa in black frames.

Sailing: navy blue, cream, tan, gray
- Paint one wall navy blue and paint the other walls a soft tan. Use cream or tan upholstered furniture, white-painted woodwork and gray accents. Frame some nautical flags and hang model boats on molding ledges.

Art gallery: tan, cream, silver, black
- Paint the walls a soft tan. Use all white upholstery furniture, silver tables, and shelving with black frames and accents.

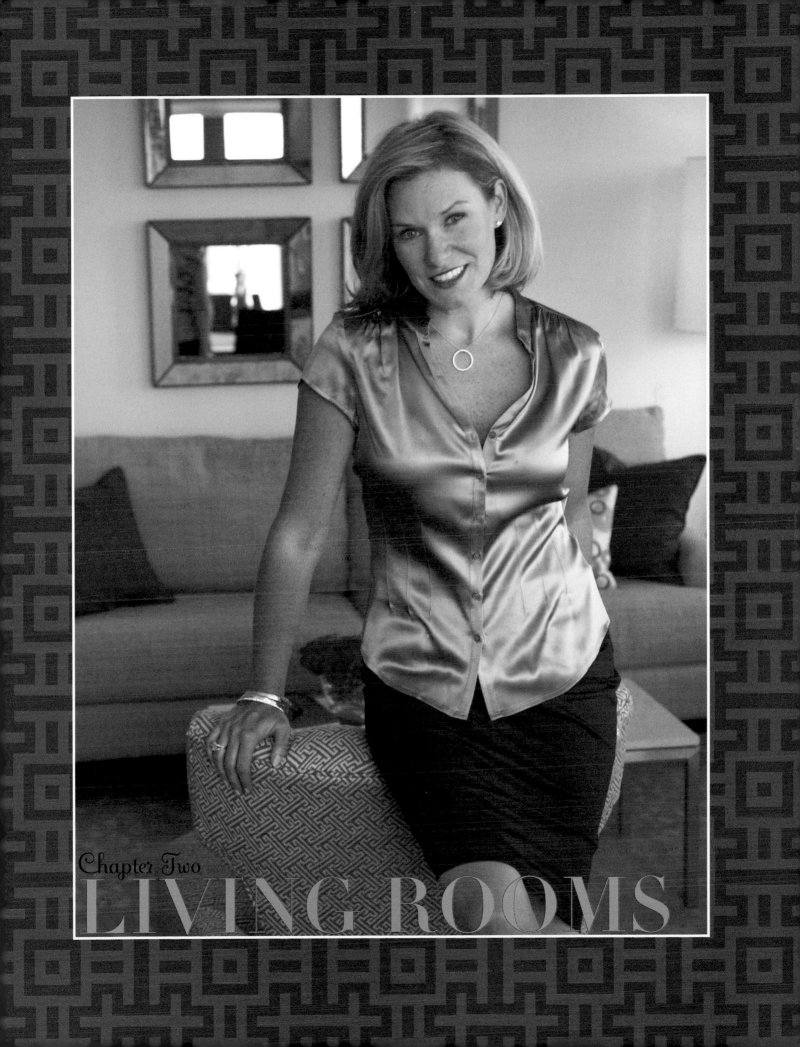

Chapter Two
LIVING ROOMS

We tend to spend many of our waking hours in our living

rooms, and we are most likely to express our personalities through their design. In small spaces they frequently serve double duty as offices or dining rooms. For all of these reasons, we often feel most intimidated to decorate them. This chapter will tackle some of the most common problems in designing a living room and reveal some quick fixes for even the most challenging space.

Finding Furniture to Fit Your Space

If you see a piece of furniture you like, but you don't know if it will work in your space, just take out a piece of graph paper to get a better perspective of what the space will hold! Measure the perimeter of your room, noting the placement of windows and doors, and draw the specs on paper. Then measure the dimensions of the furniture to see what can actually fit into the space. Keep in mind when you're laying out your space that you typically want to allow 30 to 36 inches of space between pieces of furniture for people to comfortably walk through.

I find it helpful to look at the room as a whole on a piece of paper and have cutouts of the furniture so that I can move them around and find the layout that works best for the room. I know this sounds scary, but don't worry, it's so easy once you get started. For a complete overview of working with graph paper, layouts, and furniture proportions, see How to Measure Your Space and Use Graph Paper for Layouts on page 40.

Creating Conversation Areas

It's tricky to figure out how to fit all of your furniture in your living room, keep a good flow, and maximize

We want to talk to people in an intimate setting that's a conversation area; what we don't want is to have to shout from one side of the room to the next.

seating. So when you're working with furniture in small spaces, keep my motto, "when less is more," in mind. Too much furniture—especially oversized furniture with big arms—can crowd the room and still not solve your seating problems. Think in terms of creating *conversation areas:* A loveseat and two small ottomans, or two chairs, might serve better than one large sofa. Usually no more than two people sit on a sofa at one time anyway. Think about your parties and see if that's true for you. I bet it is!

They are called "living rooms" for a reason—we design them based on how we live!

When you're shopping for a sofa, be sure to measure the overall depth as well as the length of the sofa; a 42-inch-deep sofa will occupy a lot more square footage than a 36-inch-deep sofa. If you want to make a bolder statement, you can always go hog wild and buy an incredibly long sofa that extends from one wall all the way over to another wall—just make sure it's not deeper than 36 inches. You won't have room on either side of the sofa for end tables and lamps, but you can mount a swing-arm lamp on the walls on either side that will provide reading and ambient light. It's a more contemporary look, and if you entertain a lot this might be just what you're looking for!

Chairs placed side-by-side serve the same purpose as a sofa, but visually more light and air pass through so it doesn't feel as crowded.

{How to Measure Your Space and Use Graph Paper for Layouts}

I really enjoy the layout process. It's challenging and you have to open up your mind and be willing to try all sorts of configurations. It's trial and error but much easier to play around with furniture bits on a piece of paper than physically moving around all your furniture to see what works.

It's so important to measure your space correctly and have accurate layouts for your rooms at the beginning of any design project. But it's even more crucial when you're creating a design scheme for a small space, because absolutely every inch counts! Here's how to get started in creating your optimum layout so you can capitalize on the space you have.

Size Up the Room

- Start by measuring the perimeter of the room—this means wall-to-wall as well as the door and window

frames, windows, and any niches, built-in cabinetry, and closet doors. Begin with a plain piece of paper and rough out the shape of the room (the overhead view) and put the measurements in to simply get it all down on paper.

- I prefer to write measurements in feet and inches rather than only in inches. This saves time calculating the actual footage later on (simply divide the inches by 12). For example, you measure one wall that's 89 inches long, so you write down 7 feet 4 inches, then there's a 42-inch-wide doorway, so you write down 3 feet 6 inches.

- When measuring the doorways be sure to measure the area inside the door jamb and casing. This is

As a designer I have a book that has little pieces of furniture that I use for my layouts, but just know that little pieces cut to your furniture size on graph paper work just as well.

a crucial measurement, because you'll need to double-check that any furniture you buy will actually fit through the doorways! You may also want to look at the halls or nooks that lead into rooms and make sure that armoires, sofas, and other bulky items will have enough clearance and be able to make the turn into the room.

· Measure the wall areas above and below your windows; there may be an opportunity for built-in storage or shelving in these areas.

· Measure the height of your window frames and the height of the ceiling.

· Now get some graph paper that is ¼-inch scale, so that each little square will equal 1 foot (12 inches).

· Using a ruler draw your measurements for each wall, window, and doorway onto the graph paper, with

It's funny—when my clients see my layouts for their space the first time, they say they never would have come up with them. If you're stumped on where to start, look at layouts in design magazines—they'll help get you up and running.

the squares as your footage guide. For example, if you're starting with the wall you measured at 7 feet 4 inches, you draw a straight line for 7 squares and then a third of a square to represent the 4 inches.

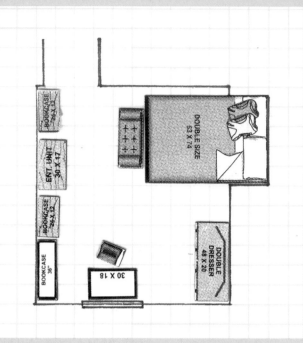

Here you can see I placed the head of the bed inside a double closet; you can still use the shelving above the bed but you gain valuable square footage.

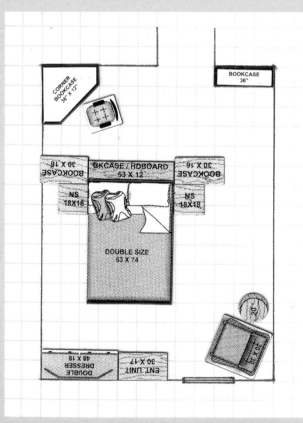

Here I placed a tall bookshelf at the head of the bed to act as a divider between the sleeping area and the desk work space.

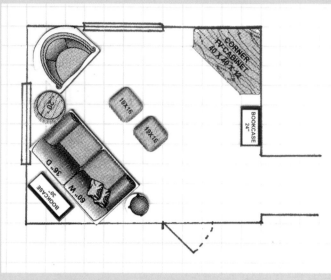

If you have a corner cabinet for your television, to optimize viewing and maximize space you may want to position your sofa kitty corner with a console table behind it, which can hold a lamp. Store less used seasonal items behind and below the sofa back corner.

- When drawing a doorway on the graph paper, draw a dash both where the doorway frame begins and ends and leave the area in between open (with no line on the graph paper). When you're laying out your furniture, this open space will tell you not to place your sofa or bed in front of the doorway!

- Draw double lines for windows on the graph paper, because you may be able to place furniture in front of the windows. Sometimes you may want to work a layout around a great view or, conversely, bright afternoon sunlight may stream into a TV room, which lets you know not to place your sofa facing that direction.

Size Up your Furnishings

- Just as you measured the dimensions of your room on graph paper, now you're going to draw your furniture. If you don't have your furniture yet, this is a great way to figure out what size furniture you *should* buy.

- This really is as simple as measuring and recording on a piece of plain paper the width, depth, and height of chairs, sofas, beds, tables, and anything else you'll be incorporating into your space.

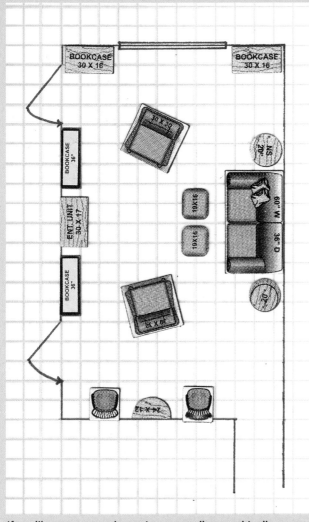

If you like a more open layout in your small space, this allows you to pass in between the chairs and the sofa, and the ottomans on casters can easily be moved instead of the standard coffee table.

- Now take out your graph paper and start drawing little boxes to represent your pieces of furniture. For example, if you have two living room chairs that are each 36 inches wide and 36 inches deep, you'll draw two boxes on the graph paper that are 3 squares by 3 squares. If your sofa is 84 inches long and 36 inches deep, you'll draw a box on the graph paper that's 7 squares by 3 squares. Be sure to write in the middle of the boxes what pieces of furniture they are meant to represent. You'll most likely be able to draw all your furniture onto one piece of graph paper, and it doesn't matter in what order you draw them.

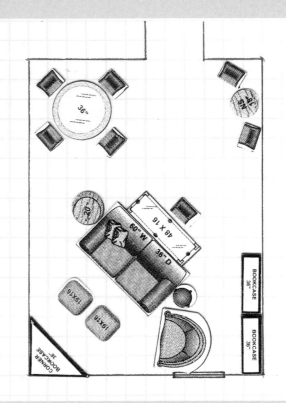

This is a great example of "floating" your sofa out into the middle of the room. The desk is positioned behind the sofa and you are really capitalizing on all the square footage, whereas if you had all the furniture pushed up against the walls, you wouldn't have room for everything and you'd waste the middle of the room by not using it!

- With a pair of scissors, cut out all of the little boxes of furniture and set them aside.

- Pull out the room layout that you drew on graph paper and start to position the little furniture boxes in the areas in the room where you think they might work. Again, keep in mind that you need to allow 30 to 36 inches between pieces of furniture so that you can comfortably walk through. For example, you don't want to set a coffee table 12 inches in front of a wall unit. Instead you want to set the coffee table about 30 to 36 inches away so that you can pass between the two pieces of furniture without feeling as if you are squeezing through!

- The trickiest part of laying out a room is getting started, but continue trying out different arrangements with your furniture pieces. If you need a little inspiration, look through interior design magazines for some layout ideas.

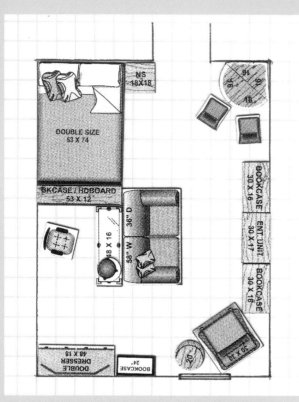

This is a good example of using your furniture as room dividers; the sofa delineates the office space, and the bookcase at the foot of the bed separates the sleeping area. Also, keep in mind that casters are a great way to keep chairs and furniture mobile in such tight quarters!

Size Up Your Perfect Area Rug

- As you're looking at your overall layout and where you want to place your furniture, see how much room you have for an area rug. Keep in mind that the larger the rug, the more spacious your room will seem, so get as large a rug as possible.

- Count each square on the graph paper as a foot, and this will give you the exact size of the rug you need to buy.

- I like to have about 14 to 16 inches of wood floor (if you have one) showing around the perimeter of the rug. This allows you to get credit for having a wood floor, but the rug is sizable enough to make your room feel welcoming and inviting. Some people prefer to see more of the floor around the rug; just be sure not to use a rug that's too tiny or it will chop your room in half and make the space look much smaller.

- Also, you have my permission *not* to have all four legs of your sofa or end tables (if they are placed up against a wall) on your area rug. It's okay to have the rug under the front two legs and have the back two legs on an exposed wood floor.

When using an area rug, you can still allow some of the bare floor to show (about 12 to 14 inches is perfect), but make sure the rug isn't too small or it will make your space seem smaller!

Average Furniture Sizes

If you're looking to buy some furniture and you don't have exact measurements yet, here are the average sizes of some common pieces you might be buying. These are general sizes and not specific small-scale pieces, but keep in mind that tons of retailers have lines of furniture designed especially for small spaces, so these are just to get you started.

- **Sofa**: 84 inches wide by 36 inches long
- **Chair**: 36 inches wide by 36 inches long
- **Coffee table**: 24 inches deep by 48 inches long
- **End table**: 22 inches wide by 22 inches deep
- **Wall unit**: 60 inches wide by 20 inches deep
- **Rectangular dining table**: 30 inches deep by 70 inches long
- **Round dining table**: 36, 54, or 60 inches in diameter
- **Dining chair**: 24 inches wide by 28 inches deep
- **Buffet**: 64 inches wide by 20 inches deep
- **King bed**: 76 inches wide by 79 inches long
- **Queen bed**: 60 inches wide by 79 inches long
- **Full/Double bed**: 53 inches wide by 74 inches long
- **Twin bed**: 38 inches wide by 74 inches long
- **Nightstand**: 20 inches deep by 26 inches wide
- **Dresser**: 54 inches wide by 18 inches deep

Redecorating a Preexisting Space

If you are in the position to redecorate and not simply reconfigure, buy furniture that facilitates creating different spaces within your living room. Chaises are unpredictable, which is refreshing, and they can lend themselves to any number of different seating arrangements depending on their size and shape. A long, narrow chaise can also double as a room divider if, for instance, you want to create different living and dining spaces within one room.

Libby-ism

An empty space looks smaller than a furnished space; it's hard to believe, but it's true! Keep this in mind when you're moving into a new space or looking to rent/buy a space … be sure to imagine what its potential might be!

Sectional sofas work well in a small space, because their configuration is interchangeable, giving you multiple seating options instead of forcing you to work around one clunky set piece. Nevertheless, since the sofa will probably be the largest piece of furniture in your room, make sure it's well proportioned. Measure carefully before you buy!

Ottomans are wonderfully versatile and can help you use your space in more than one way. Consider using two small ones as a substitute for a larger coffee table. Casters, wheels that screw into the legs of your furniture so items like chairs and ottomans can be moved around easily, are an option if you want the ottomans to double as extra seating. Plus, many ottomans have removable cushion tops for interior storage. If you find an ottoman you really love, but

Left: Storage ottomans are so useful; look for ones that are on casters so they can easily be moved where you need them.

Right: Nesting tables are a versatile choice because the smaller tables below can be pulled out when you need a mobile table surface in another area.

it doesn't have wheels, just buy some small casters at a home improvement store and put them on yourself.

Nesting tables make perfect end tables. They usually come in threes with a large table, a medium table, and a small table; the medium table stacks under the larger one, and the smaller table fits beneath the medium table. Nesting tables are small but expandable, providing additional table space if you need it. Plus, you can easily move them to another area of your space as necessary. If you don't want to buy nesting tables, you can create your own version by placing a small cube ottoman on casters underneath an end table that has legs and an open base; the ottoman can be pulled out as seating or used as another small table to hold a tray.

You can also easily and inexpensively create your own storage side table by putting a round tabletop over a sturdy bin. Store seasonal items or decorations in the bin and then cover the top with a textured table-

cloth, which will not only look great but also conceal the fact that it's really used for storage as well as an end table. Or stack old picnic baskets on top of each other to create a small, good-looking side table that has plenty of storage.

If you have open side tables or lamp tables (they don't have drawers or a cabinet below), buy some attractive baskets that will fit underneath them to hold items you use less frequently, such as purses, holiday decor, or extra bedding and towels.

A Multipurpose Living Room

Often you need one large room to do double duty and serve as two (or sometimes three) rooms. Your living room may have to house your dining area and your office space as well. You can divide the space with your layout, the furniture you choose, paint on the walls, and color.

Think of the back of your sofa as a divider; a desk, console table, or pair of chairs facing out from behind it can allow you to utilize the center of your room more effectively.

Above: Even in a large space, people often have their living room and dining room in the same area. Don't forget to allow for enough room for people to pull the dining chairs out from the table when they need to sit.

Right: If you have a long narrow space, you may be able to set a sofa at the end of your bed or in front of your bed, as the designers of this studio did. This layout works well because when you're sitting on the sofa watching TV, you're not facing or seeing the bed.

Break It Up with Bookcases

Don't be afraid to float your bookcases in the middle of the room; they can separate and define a space that needs to serve more than one purpose. Just be sure to use open shelving, which will keep an airy feel in your room. Place beautiful objects on them to provide punches of color and create that sense of openness. Remember, however, to arrange accessories and accent items in threes! Two of anything is too little and four is too much; this is true with vases, candlesticks, and just about anything. I wish I could tell you exactly *why* this is true, but I can't . . . it just is. (My mom is an interior designer and she taught me about styling things on shelves in threes and she was right! Always listen to your mother.) Have some fun and create the unexpected!

Rugs to the Rescue!

You can also visually divide and define multiple living areas in one room by using different rugs to give a separate identity to each space. Just be sure that your rugs aren't too small—the larger the rug, the bigger your room will appear. A small rug in a small space looks like a postage stamp; it chops up the space and makes it seem a little more cluttered, whereas a large rug gives you the feeling of expansiveness. Light-colored rugs will also make your room feel more spacious than darker rugs.

Sliding Doors and Screens as Separators

Sliding doors on sliding tracks hung from the ceiling are more expensive than some other options, but they can create rooms with real privacy and give you the added bonus of being able to be opened whenever you want one large room. They can be made out of wood or, even better, frosted glass or reinforced Plexiglas, which will still allow natural light into the room. If you want them to become a focal point or more of a design element, consider covering the door with an interesting wallpaper or mirror panels.

Another way to break up a long room or open space is with free-hanging frosted Plexiglas/plastic panels, which can be mounted to the ceiling with heavyweight picture wire. This may be a better option if you are renting and need something temporary, and don't want to mount sliding door hardware on your ceiling. Hang the panels 16 inches down from the ceiling, leaving a little space between each one (about 5 inches); this will allow light and air to pass through while dividing the room. For a more contemporary look and a fun way to update your existing style, get creative with the panels and attach some sheer linen with spray-mount glue. This will give the panels a little added texture without blocking any natural light.

Folding screens are more versatile than sliding doors and can provide hidden storage. Outfit them with casters, and they will be much easier to maneuver in your small space. Some folding screens even have

Above: Sliding doors with frosted glass separate your space but still let in natural light.

Above: This screen has a casual feel to it and the woven detail allows light to pass through, so it doesn't feel too heavy.

spaces to frame photographs, and those look great with black-and-white family photos or pictures from a favorite vacation.

Vertical Space

A raised platform floor is another great way to define a living area from a dining area (or office). If you install a door where the step up is, you can use the space below the platform for storing seasonal items. This is a more involved project that requires a contractor, but if you're about to remodel, this can add some valuable storage space. Kids in dorm rooms have been thinking vertically and building sleep lofts for years!

Right: This wrought-iron radiator cover adds a great design element to a living room; it's an unusual piece but it can work well with different styles.

Finding a Place for the TV

If you have one long room that serves more than one purpose—say a living room and a bedroom—and you have a flat-screen television (lucky you!), consider mounting it on the wall in the center of the room with a swivel bracket. The mounting bracket will allow you to tilt or turn the TV completely in both directions. If you have a

larger, deeper TV that needs to rest on a shelf, simply put it on a swivel base; this will enable you to turn it so you can enjoy watching TV in these two "separate" spaces. And, if you enjoy watching television in bed, just make sure you place the TV in a spot where you can watch it from both your sofa and your bed.

Mixing Furniture to Enlarge a Room

If your living room is tiny (and depressing), you can achieve a cool design that will make it appear larger by mixing and matching furniture pieces. In other words: Don't buy furniture in "sets." An entire set of pieces, while looking fabulous in the store, often results in too much furniture for a small space. Try using one piece—the table, the chairs, or the sofa—from the set. Whatever you buy, be sure to get the dimensions of each piece and incorporate them in your layout.

When you combine all different styles of furniture, everything from antiques, to 1950s mod pieces, to new contemporary items, you begin to create your own eclectic mix and craft your own personal style. I'm not sure where in the interior design rule book it says that each room must reflect just one style; I'm giving you permission to mix together the pieces you love, and I guarantee you'll design a space you truly will want to spend time in!

Work to mix and match different styles of wood, glass, and upholstery in your living room, too; this will add depth to a small area. (And yes, that means it's okay to even mix different colors of stained wood!) Combine several different textures, such as silk,

Top left clockwise: Mixing textures, glass, and interesting fabrics keeps your space from looking too "cookie-cutter."

Next: Here I mixed wood/chrome lamps, soft upholstery, and a woven palm table with a glass top to create a casual yet focused design. Remember to mix and match furniture so it doesn't look like you bought everything in "sets."

Next: This sofa looks great in the rich chocolate brown fabric, and rather than a large printed pattern, it has a small geometric pattern woven into it that makes it subtle but still interesting.

Last: The orange contrast welt on these chairs is a great added detail, and the scroll-patterned fabric works well with the Moroccan table the homeowner already had. The tufted suede ottoman adds another dimension of texture to the room.

suede, wool, linen, chenille, and cotton, to add visual interest to your space. If all the furniture in your space is one texture (cotton), it can lack dimension and feel cold. Mix surfaces on furniture as well: wood, iron, glass, mirror, rattan, and steel.

A combination of books, pictures, and small objects makes this wall unit look finished rather than haphazard.

Again, this will help create a look all your own and less "cookie-cutter."

Decorating Tips for a Small Room

When you focus smaller scale items such as accessories, books or knickknack collections in one area of your space, it gives you a more ordered and organized feeling, rather than having them everywhere. Try installing a long wall of floor to ceiling adjustable shelves; this can house everything from a bar, to a computer tower and printer, to pantry items, books, magazines, and even a flat-screen TV. You can "style" the shelves with a combination of necessary functional items (office supplies, photo-storage boxes, stationary) as well as decorative items (vases, picture frames, small art objects) to keep it looking chic. You can paint or stain the shelves to coordinate with your existing decor, which will keep it feeling part of your overall design plan. (See Styling Like a Pro—How to Style and Arrange Items in a Wall Unit on page 75.)

If you're lacking in the artwork department, take a page (or two) from your favorite book and liven up a library or living room shelf. So often in bookcases we only display the spine of a book, but if you open up the book to a picture or illustrated pages you like, you can leave the book open and rest it on a small easel to enjoy the images for more than a cursory glance. Also, if you admire the style of a particular book cover, you can simply turn the jacket so that it faces out in the bookshelf for an eye-catching design or hit of color. If you really love the image on the covers of a few of your favorite books, try framing them; it's totally original (and inexpensive because you already have the books)! This can add an especially playful, whimsical style to a child's room. After all, what's cheerier than using children's book jackets as artwork?

If you have pieces of special or expensive fabrics, create some custom artwork by framing them in contemporary frames and hanging them on the wall in a grouping. Be bold and have some fun. When you get tired of one or two of the fabrics, it's easy and cheap to swap them out!

You can add scale to a small room by using an old (large-scale) atlas as wallpaper on one wall. You don't have to go through the headache of gluing it; for a low-commitment installation, attach it to the wall on the edges with a staple gun and then hot glue some ribbon around it to cover the staples. When you want a change or it's time to move, you simply pop out the staples. Hang shelves or pictures on top of the wallpaper to break up the pattern. This inexpensive concept can add a great design to your space!

If you like to travel, consider cutting a super large black-and-white world map (4 x 6 feet) into several 12-inch squares and framing each square in a record album frame. Hang each frame side-by-side on a wall, leaving 2 inches between each frame. When you hang the frames, be sure to position the map in its original shape/form (it's now chopped up with 2-inch increments and frames in between each section). This adds a large-scale, elegant feel to a small-scale room. This technique also

works well with kid's posters, landscapes, large botanicals, or any large print you want to showcase in a fresh, new way.

You can use drapes on the windows to change the overall look and feel of your small room. Pick a fabric you love—a crisp toile, chocolate brown silk, rich red velvet, or an airy, creamy sheer. Suspend the drapes from the very top of the room—where the ceiling meets the wall—all the way to the floor. Mount them so that they stack down the wall rather than hang down inside the window. Hanging drapes on the outside of a window frame and stacking them on the wall creates the appearance of a larger window, and prevents blocking natural light.

I took these pictures of a cool looking bench with my digital camera, printed them off my computer in black and white, and framed them with wide white mattes and simple gallery frames. When they are all grouped together, they look like an expensive series of photographs.

Libby's before and afters:

Before: These windows were narrow, and the harsh lines made the room feel cold.

After: By hanging the drapes all the way up to the ceiling and letting them "stack" (see glossary) on the wall on either side of the window frame rather than inside the window frame, it makes the window seem larger. The woven bamboo shade helps cover in the area between the top of the window frame and the ceiling.

Hey look! I'm hanging drapes up to the ceiling . . . you should too!

Full-height drapes visually draw your eye up, creating the illusion of higher ceilings and thus a larger space. For most rooms with standard ceiling heights, you simply need to buy a 96-inch drapery panel instead of the 84-inch panel . . . an easy change with dramatically different results.

In front of a window, create an instant window seat by removing the legs from a dining room sideboard (a long dining room chest with legs that has storage for china and tableware). Simply chop off the legs and cover a foam cushion in fabric to fit the size of the top. You'll have a great little bench that also has storage!

How to Brighten Up a Dark Room

If your living room has no natural light and feels a bit like a cave, there's no use sitting there in the dark—bring in some artificial light! Using lighting effectively definitely changes the entire vibe of a room, and you can watch it transform from cold and unfeeling to warm and inviting. Recessed lighting can work better than a chandelier, because it spreads light more evenly throughout a room. But be sure to put the lights on a dimmer and don't use fluorescent bulbs unless you want your room to feel like your fifth-grade science lab!

These floor-to-ceiling drapes allowed me to capitalize on the great ceiling height of this nook. They helped achieve an airy, open feeling . . . not to mention elegant!

Glass can work with all textures. Some people think of it as too modern, but here it's paired with a woven palm leaf table and it's "beachy" but cool!

This black and cream palette feels rich rather than heavy because of the openness of the glass and iron table.

Here, a creative designer salvaged some architectural column supports, put pieces of glass on top, and created two small tables that work better than one large coffee table.

Remember to make the most of the light you do have: Avoid using skirted sofas and chairs. Legs on furniture allows light to come through the bottom and feel less clunky. For the same reason, use glass tops on coffee tables, end tables, and dining tables. Solid table tops block the light and can absorb too much space.

Lamp Light

Sometimes overhead lighting isn't an option (if your home isn't already wired in the ceiling). If that's the case, try an assortment of table lamps—enough to bring light into the corners of your room. And don't be afraid to use big ones! People think that a small space needs small lamps, but actually the opposite is true—larger lamps add height and scale to a small room, making it feel less constricting. If you already have lamps but you want to give them a little face-lift, buy some new lamp shades. They are easy to find, and a crisp new shade in a cool shape like a square, rectangle, or cylinder can inexpensively update the look of lamps you already own. If you have a bunch of mismatched lamps, groovy new shades can pull them together with a more uniform look.

No matter what style you're after for your space, there are plenty of lamps in all shapes, colors, and textures, but just remember, NO SHORT LAMPS!

Floor lamps offer the perfect solution when you don't have much table space and, again, the height helps to change the perspective in a small room. But please, no torchieres; they cast light up toward the ceiling and make your space uninviting.

Picture lights are our subliminal friends in the design world, because they add softness and a chic sensibility to any space. Many times people walk into a room that feels elegant and inviting and they can't figure out why . . . it's the picture lights! Some picture lights need to be hardwired and require an electrician, but many of them

The two tall lamps on either side of this sofa add a sense of balance as well as provide light and a feeling of warmth.

If you're lacking space for a table to place a lamp on, choose a floor lamp instead. Make sure it's good and tall, then it will add scale and a sense of height to your space as well as illuminate it!

just need to be plugged in and come with a wire cover to conceal the bare cord hanging down the wall. I love these because, while they don't add any real task lighting (don't try to read a book under a picture light), they do create a warm feeling and ambience. The more traditional version is made of brass, and the more contemporary option features nickel. Don't worry if you feel like your artwork isn't important enough to be illuminated; you're really using it as an excuse to add another layer of light in your space, which will make it feel more sizeable.

You can also mount picture lights on top of shelving units to add drama and illuminate the items in the unit. Instead of picture lights, you can also use a plug-in desk lamp, the kind you can angle with a metal shade. You can place it on top of a wall unit

or on the top shelf, and let it cast a glow down the front of your shelves. This especially helps if you rent your house or apartment, or don't want to drill into your wall unit; it will give you the same effect, and it's as easy as turning on a lamp!

You can even create your own mirror with a little imagination. Salvage an old door that has glass window panes and replace the glass sections with mirror. Lean it up on a wall next to your sofa behind an end table or lean it on a wall near a window. It acts as a cool architectural detail, and the mirror will reflect daylight as well as lamplight at night.

You can also make a "crown molding" mirror, using 6- to 7-inch strips of mirror. Mount them on the wall where the wall meets the ceiling. The mirrors will reflect light and make it seem as though your ceilings are higher.

The Magic of Mirrors

Mirrors reflect any light already in the room, so choose large mirrors and use as many of them as often as possible. It will amaze you to see how much they open up a room. Find 12-inch-square mirrors at your local home improvement store and set them on your table or buffet when you entertain. They will create light and expansiveness, especially when coupled with glowing candles.

{ Living Room Quick Tips }

Here are some quick tips to get your living room organized and looking fab:

- Get a long, skinny slab of marble, or several 12-inch-square stone, ceramic, or terra-cotta tiles and lay them on top of your old-fashioned pipe radiator—they will withstand the heat as well as add more tabletop space to your room. If you have a newer top-vent radiator, add marble shelves as connectors between the radiator and the walls on either side of it.

- If you don't have floor space for an end table, and you have a sitting chair next to a wall, mount white Formica shoe stackers to the wall to act as shelves or a small area to rest a drink, book, and little lamp. Instead of a traditional side table, stack up three or four antique suitcases to create a low end table. You'll have hidden storage for linens or seasonal items as well as a place to set down a drink and a book.

These antique suitcases work well as an end table, and there's tons of storage inside!

If you have lots of great big coffee table books, put them to work as a side table by stacking them on top of a plant dolly/stand outfitted with casters. It's a mobile table with great hits of color from the books!

- Benches can perform double duty as bookcases if you stack them on top of each other. Start by buying three picnic benches in various lengths that have a bottom support (this will act as an additional shelf). Center the benches on top of one another, and, if you want them to be permanent, secure them with wood glue. If you choose not to secure them, you can use them as additional seating when you entertain guests or a spot to put food and drinks.

- Stack your largest oversize coffee-table books on a plant dolly/stand that has casters. Include as many as possible (almost up to 18 inches high); it can easily be moved and it will also double as a small side table.

- Buy hanging fabric shoe-storage organizers and use a staple gun to attach them to the insides of your wall unit cabinet doors to hold small items like remote controls, matches, and cable guides.

- Make the most of the space above and below windows. Add a 1 x 4 inch board to the top of a window

Look to the insides of your cabinet doors as an opportunity to stow things away and keep yourself organized. Give everything its own spot to live and you'll keep clutter under control.

wallpaper with paste before smoothing it into place.

· If you're not a plant person, get a few tall (3- to 4-foot), clear glass cylinder vases. Fill them with modern orbs made from moss or anything green. It's a more modern way to incorporate some greenery into your space than the standard plant route! They are actually dried, but they retain their green color for a few years. (I'm not a big fan of dried flowers or wreaths that look faded and dead—it feels counterproductive when you are trying to add *life* to your space!)

· Whenever possible, hang speakers on your wall rather than allow them to take up valuable floor space.

frame to create a ledge for dishes or pictures. Mix crates and storage cubes to capitalize on the 18 to 22 inches of space usually found below a window.

· Create a cozy sitting nook by incorporating seating into your storage wall. Simply use a small bench or settee in the middle of a grouping of shelves. It's almost like creating a window seat.

· Line the back of a shelving unit or bookcase with wallpaper to make art and accessories stand out. Cut the paper to size, test the fit, and then coat the

I love these green moss balls. They look cool and modern but they still give that punch of green that every space needs!

If you can mount your speakers on the wall, it's a great way to free up table space. These speakers are so small you barely even notice them!

LIBBY'S TRICKS OF THE TRADE

Forget "Matchy-Matchy"—How to Use Contrast in Your Space

One of the best tools to use when designing your space is color contrast. You may be asking yourself, "Self, what does color contrast really mean?" Well, I'll tell you . . . it's uniting the opposite ends of the color spectrum, pairing light tones with dark tones to add visual interest. Interior designers use this secret technique to combine contrasting colors in a room where most other people would say, "Will that go with everything else in the room" or "Is it going to match?" Sometimes when everything "matches," or is in the same color tone, the room can look a little blah. But if you bring in a hit of a lighter or darker tone, it can add depth and dimension to a space, as well as a little personality!

These silver-plated shells really shine on the dark wood tabletop.

Here's how to begin using color contrast like a pro:

- If you have furniture covered in light fabrics, consider painting your walls a darker color. This will highlight what you have and add depth and dimension. (And vice versa: If you have furniture in darker tones, keep the colors on your wall lighter.)

- Consider the color on the floor as much as the color on the walls or furniture. If you have dark furniture, opt for light floor coverings; if it's all dark it can visually "weigh down" your space—you don't want it to feel like a black hole in there!

- Be conscious about the lampshades you choose; if your walls are light, consider using a black or chocolate brown shade—it will give you a nice pop of color in front of your pale wall.

- With artwork, look at your wall color and choose the opposite tone for the frame. If you have dark walls, use a white or silver frame, and if you have light walls, use a dark wood or black frame.

This dark china cabinet pops in front of the light wall.

These rich, dark frames and lampshades look fantastic on the pale yellow walls.

If your walls are dark, use light lampshades and if your walls are light, consider using a darker shade (just not if it's where you sit and read—you want to use light shades to get the maximum amount of light from a reading lamp).

- When you accessorize, look at the tone of your shelving units and furniture and select accessories in opposite color tones. If you have white shelving, use colorful or dark items (vases, books, candlesticks, picture frames) that will pop out visually from the unit. If you have dark shelving, use lighter, paler items and silver-toned accessories; you'll see the items so much better than if they were all dark and blended into the unit.

- Place throw pillows on sofas and chairs in the opposite tone of your upholstered furniture. With a light sofa include some dark pillows, and with a dark sofa incorporate light pillows.

- If you have a dark color on your walls, select lighter window treatments, and if you have lighter walls, go a little bolder with some darker window treatments. This applies to window shades as well as draperies. And don't be afraid to have some fun with your window treatments—they are easily changed and don't have to cost a fortune when you're ready for a new look.

Chapter Three
DINING ROOMS

The most frequent problem people encounter in their dining rooms is lack of natural light. But in small spaces dining rooms have many other problems, too. For one, they can be especially tiny. And if a dining room has to serve as a shared space, figuring out how to divide it can be tricky. Other challenges include creating a buffet or serving space and finding a storage space for certain items so that you don't have to get up and scurry into the kitchen every time someone needs something. Plus, no matter how small your dining space is, you want to be sure that it has comfortable seats (cushions are always welcome), soft and soothing lighting (no bare chandelier bulbs!), and an ambience that invites you and your guests to linger at the table. This chapter will tackle all of these problems.

How to Brighten Up a Dark Dining Room

If your dining room has "gloomy" written all over it, consider painting just *one* of the walls a dark color (a rich chocolate brown, an elegant navy blue, or a rich eggplant) or a bright, vibrant color (a chili pepper red, a warm yellow, or a citron green), which will make the walls recede visually (giving the illusion of pushing it back). Then position a large mirror on it. The rich paint will accentuate the mirror as well as add some pizzazz. Next, put a sideboard—or any table that fits—underneath the mirror with lamps on it. The mirror will reflect the lamplight, and before you know it, your dining room will be glowing.

A dining room is a great spot to try out a vibrant wall color; just be sure to add lamplight and get large artwork or a mirror up on the wall to break it up.

The rich red wall color, soft seats, and diffused chandelier light make this an inviting spot to spend an evening with friends and family. Red is a great color for a dining room because studies have shown that people actually like to eat in red rooms—it's stimulating and energetic.

Improvising a Dining Area When You Don't Have One

If you don't have an actual separate dining room, do you have a small alcove that you can convert into its own space? All you need is enough room for a small, easily expandable table that can be closed and pushed up against a wall when you're not using it.

You can make a small dining nook feel more dignified by hanging some artwork on the walls. Large artwork or a grouping of pictures will give the space a much more comfortable and distinct personality. Also, take some creative license with color on your walls to make the alcove feel like a separate room. If your alcove is truly small, a bold wall color will give it a more intimate

rather than overwhelming feel. You may want to put a rug in there as well, which can also establish the feeling of a separate space. Make sure you have a great lighting fixture with soft light—no bare bulbs—and if you have a chandelier, be sure to get small chandelier shades to cast a soft, warm glow.

Another way to add something special to your small dining area (or kitchen) is to create an inexpensive and personal piece of art by surrounding a large (5 x 4 feet) piece of corkboard with framing material or molding. Tack everything from postcards to concert tickets to party pictures to the corkboard and change them as often as you like. It will add a burst of color to your space as well as stimulate conversation at every meal—and it's fun because it's ever-changing!

Libby's before and afters:

Before: This dining nook has great natural light, but the dark wallpaper drained it and made it feel cold, not to mention the ugly ceiling fan.

After: Here you can see how the yellow wall color warmed up the space, and the new chandelier with the chandelier shades gives off a soft glow.

Before: This dining nook looks and feels like an afterthought—the wallpaper border is dated and the furniture is tired; add in some small mismatched pictures and it's a haphazard space!

After: I updated the space by adding citron green on the walls, a white dining set (this one's new but we could have even painted the one they already had white), a new chandelier with shades, and then pulled together some black and white photographs as accents. It's a fresh, new look.

Right: This was a tiny little nook that I turned into a Moroccan-style eating niche; the colorful drapes add color and coziness, and there's just enough room for the little bistro table and chairs.

Above and left: Sometimes you can dedicate an unused corner in a living room as a dining area. Large artwork above the table can help define the space and make it feel more important. These zebra chairs are eye catchers!

Cozy Dining Room Furniture

Most rectangular dining tables are at least 36 inches wide, but a narrow table will save space and can be equally effective. You can have a table as slender as 28 inches that will work beautifully as a desk and/or a dining table. A glass top is ideal for a small space, because it will allow light to filter through the room and create the feeling of more space.

Armless chairs work best in small spaces, but use cushions for comfort and to soften the ambience. If you don't have room for lots of chairs, use stackable ones that can be stored when not in use. Or take a bench from your hallway or the foot of your bed and throw cushions on it.

Far left: Don't be afraid to use different chairs at your dining table; this glass tabletop allows you to see more of the chairs than a wooden top would.

Left: The glass tabletop keeps this dining spot feeling open and airy, even in front of the chocolate accent wall.

Far left: This dining area is dramatic because of the great contrast between the black and cream color scheme. The glass tabletop keeps it from feeling too heavy, and the round lines of the chandelier shade and chair backs add a little softness.

Left: Armless chairs are a better choice for a smaller dining area because they allow you to push the chairs all the way under the table when not in use, so you free up square footage to walk around easily. Visually they also look cleaner, more open, and less busy.

Libby-ism

Things feel uncluttered when everything has its place, but things feel cluttered when every place has a thing!

table runner, or decorative box. For inexpensive centerpieces, hot glue crystal knobs to the backs of beveled, frameless mirrors. (You can usually buy a box of beveled mirror tiles at most home improvement stores.) Three of these petite, elevated mirror trays look fantastic running down the center of your dining table—they reflect daylight and candlelight, too!

If you don't have room in your dining area for a buffet cabinet, mount a long floating shelf along a wall. This will keep the space open, but you will have a place to set items that won't fit on your table while you're entertaining. The long continuous line will also give the illusion of a longer room. If the

If you'd like to create your own dining room table, a large planter can provide an inexpensive base. You can find large planters at any garden supply or home improvement store. You can choose a square wooden planter, a round cylindrical planter, or any other style that appeals to you, as long as it's at least 29 inches high, which is standard table height. Have a piece of glass cut to fit on top, either round or square, any size from 32 to 48 inches, depending on how much room you have. Then store items you use less frequently inside the planter and place something attractive on top (since you'll be looking inside the planter through the glass top), such as a neat basket, platter,

We had this one large sheer shade made to go over the chandelier and smaller shades to diffuse the light and add a neat design element; the key was using an ultra sheer, gauzy fabric to allow the maximum amount of light.

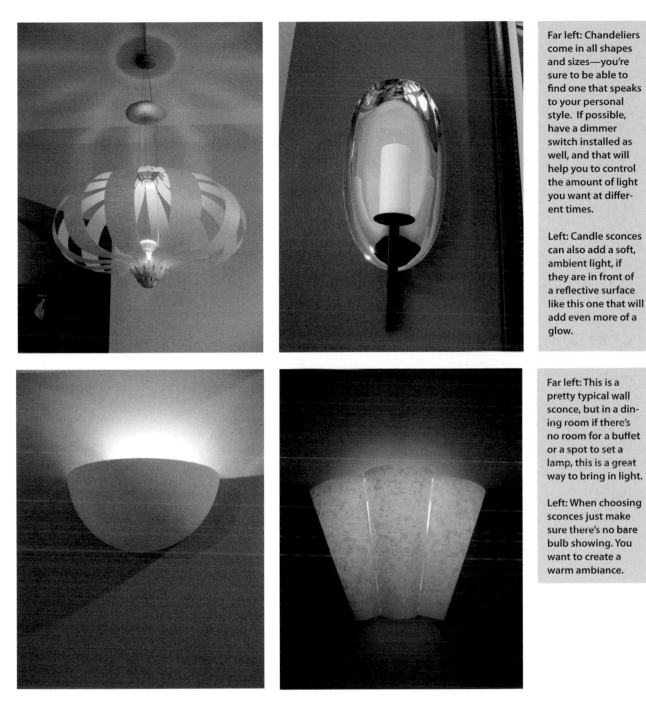

Far left: Chandeliers come in all shapes and sizes—you're sure to be able to find one that speaks to your personal style. If possible, have a dimmer switch installed as well, and that will help you to control the amount of light you want at different times.

Left: Candle sconces can also add a soft, ambient light, if they are in front of a reflective surface like this one that will add even more of a glow.

Far left: This is a pretty typical wall sconce, but in a dining room if there's no room for a buffet or a spot to set a lamp, this is a great way to bring in light.

Left: When choosing sconces just make sure there's no bare bulb showing. You want to create a warm ambiance.

shelf isn't deep enough to hold a lamp, fasten a swing-arm lamp to the wall; since you attach it directly to the wall, they won't rob you of any buffet space. A swing-arm lamp also allows you to swing the lamp out so that you can position the light exactly where you want it, while you still receive the benefit of warmer lighting because of the lamp shade.

Wall sconces are another good choice for adding style and additional lighting without stealing buffet space. While plug-in versions do exist, the majority of wall sconces need to be hardwired into the wall. You may decide it's worth the cost of hiring an electrician, because it won't take him or her very long to do.

Look for a chic rolling cart that could create a mobile bar; this one houses just about everything you could need.

This shallow shelving unit is a perfect spot for a bar with wine-glass hanging racks built into the lower shelves.

Add a welcoming feeling to your dining space by creating a floating wine-storage area. Simply attach wine-glass hanging racks underneath a 12-inch-deep shelf that you've mounted on the wall. Fill it will your glasses, dish towels, and cocktail napkins. Store your bottles of wine on top of the shelf, and you're ready for a party at a moment's notice! You can also use a salvaged (or new) metal cart with shelves and wheels as an entertainment/bar station. You can move it around, and it houses everything from wine and glasses to food and napkins. When you're not entertaining, it can store table linens and serving pieces.

You may have room for a bar or a cabinet, which could have lighting inside.

If you like to entertain but don't have room for additional seating when you don't have guests, use stacking backless stools. When you are not using them, stack them and set them in a corner with a plant, a sculpture, or stacks of coffee table books on top. They will function and look good when you need them as well as when you don't!

Consider covering one entire wall with floor-to-ceiling cabinets for extra storage and use hardware-free doors on the cabinets to make them less noticeable. By not using hardware, the cabinets will disappear into the space, and they will look like ordinary wood panels rather than storage cabinets. You can also put mirrors on the inside panels of your doors or cabinet faces for added interest and to reflect more natural light.

If you don't want to cover an entire wall with cabinets, but you need some additional storage, mount kitchen cabinets (the kind that usually hang on the wall above your countertops) low on the wall, at buffet height, so that the tops of the cabinets are about 40 inches off the ground. At this height they won't reach the floor—they will essentially be levitating—but the open area below the cabinets will give you the illusion of more space, not to mention all the storage you'll be gaining inside the cabinets! You'll most likely need to have some sort of top made, because many cabinets aren't flush and finished on the top. At buffet height, the top of the cabinets will also provide a resting place for trays, glasses, and other dining-ware items.

A Multipurpose Dining Table

If you use your dining room table only every now and then, consider making your own double-duty table. While I generally never suggest ideas that require additional help, a dining table with interchangeable legs is worth it: You will have one table that serves two purposes and requires no extra storage. Buy a large coffee table—it can be square, rectangular, or round—with legs that screw into the tabletop. (You can easily find one of these—a huge variety of chains such as Pottery Barn or Straight from the Crate carry furniture that requires assembly.) Find a local woodworker to construct four longer legs—at the standard dining table height, 29 to 30 inches high—that will also screw into the tabletop. Or, conversely, buy a dining table and have a carpenter make four shorter legs so you can use it a coffee table.

If you're one of those hardworking folks who have a home office and no room for much else, you can still create a space for friends for dinner using a desk-to-dining table. Find a small-scale dining table with wooden legs and attach locking casters to the bottom of the legs. During the day this can be your desk, near computer equipment files and paperwork. At night, stash your desk work into sturdy leather file boxes, roll your desk into the middle of the room, decorate it with flowers and candles, and kick up your heels! The file boxes can be stacked and used as a spot for someone to rest a drink, a plate of appetizers, or a small flower arrangement.

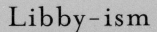

Libby-ism

If you're not a big fan of silk plants (and you travel a lot or don't really have a green thumb), use a tall, narrow urn or planter and fill it with some long, skinny twigs. This will achieve the same height element that you'd get from a tall silk tree in a corner.

Tall shelves not only give great storage but they can also double as an effective room divider. Shown at the top is one side of the shelf acting as storage for the living room area. At the bottom the shelf serves as storage for the kitchen and dining room area.

Dining Room Dividers

A great way to divide a living room and dining room is with two tall, side-by-side open shelving units. But you can take it one step further by dry mounting two posters onto foam core board and hanging the posters on alternating sides of the shelving unit. It's a dramatic look that separates the space yet still feels open. Plus it offers storage space for serving pieces in the dining room on one side and a display area for items in the living room on the other side.

LIBBY'S TRICKS OF THE TRADE

Styling Like a Pro—How to Style and Arrange Items in a Wall Unit

Accessories definitely transform your space from cold to chic, but it's tricky to find the right balance between looking comfy and lived-in versus cluttered and cramped. A little can go a long way when it comes to styling a wall unit with a combination of books, pictures, and objects. I'm happy to report that a few tried-and-true ways can help you achieve the perfect placement.

So often people tell me that they don't know how to "arrange" things. They want that cool look they see in catalogs and home furnishing stores, but they're not sure how to execute it themselves. If you want to pull off a similar design in your own space, find a shelving unit that you think looks fantastic in a catalog or magazine and simply try to duplicate it. Or, for a step-by-step game plan, read on . . .

- Take everything out of your shelving/wall unit. This will give you a fresh start as well as encourage you to clear out some items that need to go (like that mug from Disneyland that you've had since third grade).

- Separate objects into piles: a book pile, a vase pile, a candlestick pile, a framed picture pile. This gives you perspective and allows you to begin using each pile as a layer.

- You'll most likely want to slim down the piles. Donate any old paperbacks and only hold onto the good-looking hardcover books; ditch the funky candlestick with all the wax melted on it. This process will allow you to rethink the items you already have.

- Now slowly begin grouping books together in threes and fives and place them alternately lying down and standing up on various shelves of the wall unit. If you have some books with beautiful covers, stand them up with the covers facing out; this will add depth and dimension. Do *not* put books on every shelf—skip a few here and there to allow some open space. The books will serve as the backbone or building blocks of your look.

The best way to begin is to start with a completely empty unit.

Begin with books and try arranging them in vertical and horizontal groupings.

• Now it's time to make it personal and incorporate a few photographs; family pictures will add warmth to your space, or you can use black-and-white pictures of objects or landscapes for an extra hit of upscale style. You can use 8 x 10s and let them stand alone on a shelf, or you can rest smaller frames, such as 4 x 6s and 5 x 7s, on top of some books that are lying on their sides . . . now your unit is starting to come to life!

• Stand back and look at the overall mixture of items. Does one section seem heavier or more crowded than another? Does one section appear unbalanced? Move pieces around one at a time until it begins to feel even, and remember that it doesn't have to be symmetrical (one book on this side and one book on the opposite side). It just needs to feel balanced!

• It you have the space, consider arranging a small green plant or two in your wall unit. Green plants are our subliminal friends in a small space (or any space for that matter). They give us a grounded feeling and add that little zip of color that always feels like the perfect finishing touch!

• Now comes the hard part . . . keep the shelves balanced and avoid junking them up with all kinds of stuff (like the mug your son brings you from Disneyland)!

Next add in a few small art objects, vases, and so on.

• If you have a shelf that has more vertical space, consider creating a little makeshift bar. Use a neat tray and fill it up with all sorts of liquor, carafes, and bar accessories; it will anchor your shelving unit as well as put it to good use when you entertain!

• Next, start to add in vases, candlesticks, and small decorative boxes. Place them on shelves alone or next to a few vertical books and don't forget to alternate shelves. Again, start out adding items sparsely—your wall unit will fill up before you know it!

Stand back and see if there's one side that looks heavier than the other; keep moving things around until it looks and feels balanced. Good job!

Now add in some framed photographs.

Chapter Four
KITCHENS

Kitchens in small spaces come in many forms, ranging from a dark room with very few cabinets, minimal counter space, and maybe a small dining nook, to an even smaller alcove with half a refrigerator and some hot plates (most likely in a studio apartment). Okay, maybe the second example sounds a little drastic, but if you enjoy cooking and your kitchen is tiny it can feel like that.

The challenges of a small kitchen stem from two major issues: insufficient storage and the absence of light (with a lack of personality coming in as a close third). Having your kitchen items pile up with no place to keep them can make the room feel overcrowded and therefore even smaller than usual. The recipe is simple: Whittle down the items you need to the bare essentials, toss in a pinch of creative storage options, add a dash of inexpensive lighting ideas, throw in some fun design elements, and you've added a little spice to your space! I have some great solutions to your kitchen problems, so let's get cookin'!

Bring in the Light!

It's not unusual for small spaces to have tiny, windowless kitchens—if you're lucky enough to have a separate kitchen—and if you want to perk up your cooking area, begin by adding more light. Think in terms of layers of light: task lighting to illuminate your work space (pendants or angled tracks) and ambient, indirect light to add overall brightness (recessed cans, under–wall-cabinet lighting, or ceiling fixtures) that will also make your space look larger.

Track Lighting

When I walk down the street in New York City at night, I often look up into apartments and see how many people live with ceiling-mount overhead light fixtures, which look so cold and uninviting. Most people would probably be shocked to learn that track lighting emits a much warmer quality of light and would make their space feel so much more homey and comfortable.

The combination of recessed ceiling cans, pendants and under-the-cabinet lighting adds layers of light to this small kitchen and makes it feel bigger.

Right top: Track lighting is great when it's angled strategically to illuminate multiple areas.

Right bottom: Track lights come in all shapes and sizes. There's a lot more to choose from these days than those plain, huge cans from the 1980s.

Track lights work well for kitchens, because they can be angled to illuminate every nook and cranny and can be put on dimmers. What's more, they are inexpensive and readily available at most home improvement stores. You will need an electrician to install them, but it's so worth it!

Under-Wall-Cabinet Lighting

In addition to lighting up your counter space, under-wall-cabinet lighting adds depth and dimension to your kitchen and creates practical light for your countertops and cooking area. You'll feel as if you have more work space, because you can see it better, and it will be much warmer and more comfortable.

You can easily find under-wall-cabinet-lighting kits at any home improvement store. Simply install them underneath your wall cabinets so that they shine down onto your countertops, backsplash, and work space. Halogen surface-mount fixtures are inexpensive and readily available at home improvement stores, too. Some can be plugged in, while others must be hard-wired, so make sure you find the right one to suit your needs. If you can see the fixture or the actual bulbs and it bothers you, you can hide the lights by attaching some molding (there are dozens of styles to choose from) to the bottom of the cabinets.

Libby's before and afters:

After: **New lighting, a new wall color, a new island, and painting their existing cabinets black was my recipe for how to update this tired kitchen.**

Before: **The wallpaper border and the overhead ceiling fan lights are a big no-no in any kitchen.**

Above: Under-cabinet lighting is crucial in any kitchen but especially in a small one.

Left: These glass mosaic tiles are actually recycled and made from old car windshields!

Middle: In a small kitchen you can mix bold colors on your backsplash because it's covering a minimal area.

Bottom: You can have fun and use great materials for your backsplash in a small kitchen because you won't need that much of it. These glass mosaic tiles steal the show!

Brighten Up Your Backsplash

The backsplash is the wall area below your wall cabinets and above your countertops, traditionally covered with some sort of waterproof material to protect it from water that splashes up from the sink and food that splatters up from the cooktop.

Backsplashes have been transformed from a utilitarian area designed to serve a purpose to an opportunity to add some great style to your kitchen. In a small kitchen you can create an aesthetically pleasing backsplash while at the same time make your space feel larger.

Add mirrors to or paint your backsplash to create light and/or a punch of color. To add some style and protect the backsplash from splatters, you can cover painted areas with frosted glass that has a glossy polished side. Light-colored ceramic or stone tiles are more expensive, but if you're in the mood to splurge they really add a wow factor to your kitchen. To create even more impact, install them on the diagonal rather than simply straight up and down. This will also make the space seem larger. You might want to apply stainless steel as your

backsplash; the reflective surface bounces so much light—and it's easy to clean!

Get Creative with Cork

Try using cork floors in your kitchen; they lighten and soften the look and feel of a small room by adding texture, and they are easy to maintain, comfortable to stand on, and noise resistant. Cork floors are also ecofriendly and available in tons of colors and can easily be installed in tiles or sheets. If your local flooring company doesn't carry cork, search online—you'll be amazed at the selection.

Simple Ways to Create More Counter Space

If you don't have enough counter space, and you need more room to chop and prep, consider hiding your appliances. Place your microwave in a cabinet, on a shelf, or on top of your refrigerator. Keep out the small appli-

ances you use most, such as your toaster and coffeemaker, and stow away less-utilized equipment, such as blenders and mixers. You'll also get the added perk of a more elegant-looking work space, because without all of these items, the counter space has a more streamlined appearance.

Many appliance manufacturers began designing for

small spaces awhile ago. I have noticed an increasing number of kitchens with two small under-the-counter refrigerators instead of one large one, which can visually overwhelm a small kitchen. I am also noticing more and more 18-inch-wide (as opposed to the standard 24-inch) dishwashers and microwave drawers. In my opinion these appliances are great investments.

Get Organized!

One of the simplest ways to achieve more space in a small kitchen is to organize your items more effectively. Here are some organization tips to help clear space on your countertops:

- Use square canisters and containers. They are more efficient than round ones and waste less space in cabinets and on counters.

- Mount a magnetic strip on the backsplash or the side of a cabinet to hold knives.

- Mount a long towel bar on the cooktop backsplash and hang a bunch of S hooks on it to hold utensils; not only will they be up on the wall, not using valuable drawer/counter space, they'll be easier to access while you're cooking! S hooks are metal hooks in the shape of an S that allow you to hang one end over a pole, while the other end can hold myriad things. (You can also mount wire baking racks to the wall and use S hooks for hanging frequently used items.)

- Cover your backsplash with magnetic chalkboard tiles that can hold kids' artwork, notes, tickets, and reminders. Magnetic hooks can keep small utensils up off the counter.

This is a simple wire baking rack, just like the one you let cookies cool on after you take them out of the oven, but mounted on the wall it becomes a grid to hang utensils on. Anyone can do this quickly and inexpensively!

- Utilize the backsplash between your counters and the bottom of your cabinets for storing items. Put in a Peg-Board or a grid from which you can hang S hooks, rails, or pull-down shelves. These items are available at any home improvement store and using them underneath your cabinets creates the perfect place to store utensils, small kitchen accessories, and spices.

- Create fun, functional kitchen storage with wooden wine crates. Visit your local wine store and ask if you can buy their empty wooden crates (many places are happy to get rid of them and will give them to you for free). They stack really well, look great, and are the perfect size to store photographs, office supplies, and seasonal items . . . and the price is right!

- Create a solid wall of hanging shelves, but mount the bottom shelf about 2 inches above your kitchen table height. Use a steel work table/office desk on casters as your dining table. When you want a dining table, it can roll out into the center of the room. When you need a desk, it can tuck in under the wall of shelving.

- Cover the face of your refrigerator or kitchen cabinets with corkboard for an inexpensive update; some appliance manufacturers offer cork when you purchase the item, or you can simply buy a sheet of cork or cork tiles from a home improvement store and glue them on using adhesive spray. You can always just use magnets, but corkboard is a perfect alternative if you have an older fridge that isn't too cool looking but you're not in a position to buy a new fabulous stainless-steel model.

- Your garage isn't the only place for commercial-grade storage—use a steel tool-storage unit for kitchen storage, too. They're economical and have ball-bearing drawers that slide easily and casters to keep the unit mobile. Designate the slim drawers to hold placemats, take-out menus, and silverware.

- Line the inside of your upper pantry doors or cabinets with Peg-Board and use small office binder clips to hold tape, coupons, memos, and rubber bands. Simply hang the metal opening of the binder clip from one of the Peg-Board hooks. You can also affix precut cork squares to the inside of your cabinet or cupboard door with adhesive spray—it's a handy spot to tack up receipts, coupons, and reminders.

- Pare down dishes and glassware to the basics and stack them on open shelves. You'll be surprised by how few plates, glasses, and bowls you use on a daily basis.

- Claim under-cabinet space by attaching screw-top jars with heavy-duty Velcro. Attach one piece of Velcro to the top of the jar cap and the other piece of Velcro to the underside of the cabinet. You can fill the jars with everything from herbs and spices to supplies like rubber bands, matchbooks, and toothpicks. Rather than take up valuable counter space, these items get to hang under your cabinet.

How to Create More Cabinet Space

If you're looking to maximize your cabinet space but don't have the room for full-depth cabinetry units, mount a wall of shallow, mirrored medicine cabinets on top of each other and side-by-side. Although shallow, they are just deep enough (about 6 inches) to hold glassware and spice jars. You'll be adding storage without consuming any square footage, and the mirrors reflect light to visually open up your space. Mirrored 26 x 20 inch cabinets are standard and available at home improvement stores. Just be sure that you can properly anchor them to the wall. The consistency in cabinet size makes this arrangement seem like a built-in, and you will have created both elegance and charm while finding more storage space.

If you have the chance to renovate or build your own kitchen, think about building your countertops higher than the standard height. Visually, it will make your kitchen appear a bit larger and more impressive. In addition you'll make life easier on your back, and you'll gain a little extra storage room underneath.

Besides finding ways to increase your cabinet space, you can also create more visually appealing cabinets. Replace your solid-wood kitchen cabinet doors with frosted-glass doors. You'll save money by replacing just the doors (rather than buying all new cabinets) but gain so much visually with the light and airy effect from the glass faces. If you can install light inside the glass cabinets, it will look over-the-top fabulous, because you will be adding another dimension of light, which will make the kitchen seem much larger.

Above: A medicine cabinet can be used in the kitchen to store a single row of glassware.

Left: Here I used an old medicine cabinet in a kitchen to store spices next to the stove.

Above: Pots and pans are space hogs, so hang them up on your wall from cup hooks or from the ceiling using a potrack.

Get Organized!

Often the key to finding more room in your cabinets is simply a matter of learning how to organize them. Here are some organization tips to maximize cabinet space:

- Use a pot rack whenever possible; pots and pans are big and bulky and take up the majority of your cabinet space. And if your ceilings are too low for a pot rack, hang your pots on your kitchen wall from simple screw-in cup hooks. It takes no time at all, frees up a ton of cabinet space, and makes grabbing a pot much easier than bending over and rifling through an overstuffed cabinet.

- It might sound obvious, but use drawer dividers. There are many different kinds available, and you will easily find dimensions to work for you. You'll fit more in your drawers, and they'll stay organized (line the drawers with those little grip rubber mats to keep everything in its proper place).

- If your kitchen has minimal cabinet space and building more cabinets is not in your budget (or allowed in your lease), consider purchasing a small-scale armoire. It can add tons of storage as well as a little personality. Be sure to outfit the interior with additional shelves; you want to maximize its potential to hold as much as possible.

- To capitalize on under-the-sink storage, add small stackable wire shelves to house cleaning supplies and detergents. You'll be using all the under-the-counter space as well as making items easier to reach.

- Use metal swing-out racks in a base corner kitchen cabinet (these racks attach to the inside of a cabinet door, and when you open the door the rack comes out). They make it easier to access cabinets in corners and make use of space that would otherwise be wasted.

- In tight kitchen cabinets or pantries, use lazy Susans for spices and commonly used cooking ingredients.

- If you have a window in your kitchen, hang a wall-mount pot rack so that it extends from the wall on one side of the window to the other. Hang it up as high as you can possibly reach the pots; you'll be utilizing the space, but the pots won't completely obstruct the view or the natural light.

- Add Peg-Board to the back of a cabinet or pantry door and use S hooks to suspend utensils, pot holders, or even shallow pots.

- Create a wall of storage in the kitchen by hanging floating shelves; china, glassware, and ceramics look fantastic out in the open and often add that extra touch of beauty or decoration to your space. Just be sure to keep the items on the shelves neat and organized—you don't want the shelving to look cluttered and messy.

- Hang a wall-mount schoolhouse book rack (the shallow racks used in kids' classrooms to store their books) to hold cookbooks, magazines, and pot holders. The bottom rack can house flat cookie sheets.

- Use a narrow console table that has shelves as an island. The lean dimensions will work better than a boxy square unit, and you'll gain storage for large pots and pans or bowls as well as add needed counter space on top.

Add an Island!

A small island can be a lifesaver in a tiny kitchen. Most people think they don't have room for one, but chances are you *do* have space for an island! You generally only need 30 inches between your counters and the island to comfortably pass through. If you can't put in a real island, use a kitchen rolling cart that has pull-out shelves and a wooden top; this multifunctional piece can serve as an island/workstation, a storage area, and a small table.

A tall white hutch looks great in this designer's kitchen. With open shelving you want to keep items neat and orderly to avoid a cluttered feeling in your room.

Mobile Islands

If you can't afford to have a real island built in your kitchen—or you'd like something more movable—you can turn an old chest of drawers, or some old wall cabinets, into a mobile island. Simply attach casters to the bottom and add a longer top so that there's a bit of an overhang. You'll gain tons of storage and be able to push it up against a wall when you're not using it.

You can also turn an old metal shopping cart into a mobile island. Find a shopping cart that has a flat top to the upper basket and a lower shelf section. Have a large piece of butcher block cut, allowing for a 5-inch overhang around three sides. It will be heavy enough that you won't need to attach it, plus you'll want to be able to move it so that you can use the area inside the cart for storage. In the front basket (you know, the place where you used to sit as a kid and dangle your legs), put three buckets to hold cooking utensils, oils, and vinegars. Hang dish towels over the handle, hang S hooks off the grate in the front to hold pot holders, and store pots and pans inside the upper basket under the butcher block. On the shelf below, place baskets to hold fruit, bottles of water, and soda.

A mobile island for the kitchen provides great storage opportunities. Don't just use the inside shelves; S hooks allow you to take advantage of the front of the cart and hang things on the outside of it as well.

LIBBY'S TRICKS OF THE TRADE

Go Green—How to Effectively Use Green Plants in Your Space
(Real or Fake!)

Some people are afraid greenery can look too country or traditional, but here you can see how cool leaves in a simple vase can look modern and updated.

I like to use tall silk trees to add a sense of height and scale to a room as well as a little life!

An incredibly important element in any space, large or small, is the presence of something green! I often find that my clients don't realize how a tall tree or a small potted plant can alter the entire feel of a room. It's almost subliminal, but it adds life and a feeling of hominess to a room. Here are some tips for adding green to your space:

If you don't have good natural light in your space, or you don't have a green thumb, use silk trees and plants—just make sure to fluff them when you get them and keep them dusted! As with most things, versions can vary in quality. Personally I like the ones that use a real tree trunk with only silk in the leaves; they look best to me.

- When you're shopping for a tree, make sure it's *tall* . . . the taller, the better . . . but make sure it's not too wide. You want the height visually because it will make your space feel bigger, but you don't want it to protrude out into your room and eat up lots of square footage.

- Steer clear of wide palms, which can take up a lot of space, and look for dracaenas and trees that have tall, skinny trunks and smaller foliage.

- When you're deciding where to place the tree or a plant, walk into your space and see if there's an empty corner on the opposite side of the room—that's probably the best place to put it.

Greenery doesn't have to be big; even the smallest little plant on a side table will have a big impact.

- With smaller plants you don't need a bunch of them—maybe two or three spread throughout your space. Consider an orchid in an entryway or on a dresser in the bedroom and a small green plant on an end table behind some pictures. That little hint of green or burst of color will do the trick!

- A more modern way to introduce green into your space is to fill a glass bowl or clear glass cylinder vase with moss-covered balls. They look chic and contemporary and give you the hit of green you need.

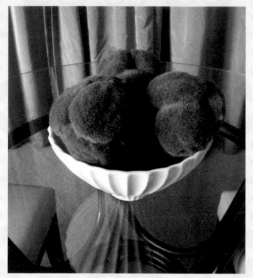

These moss-covered balls give a contemporary feel while adding that important punch of green.

- If you're not a big fan of silk trees, consider using a grouping of tall twigs in a tall planter. You won't get the hit of green, but you will get the same visual effect of something tall in your corner that makes your space feel larger.

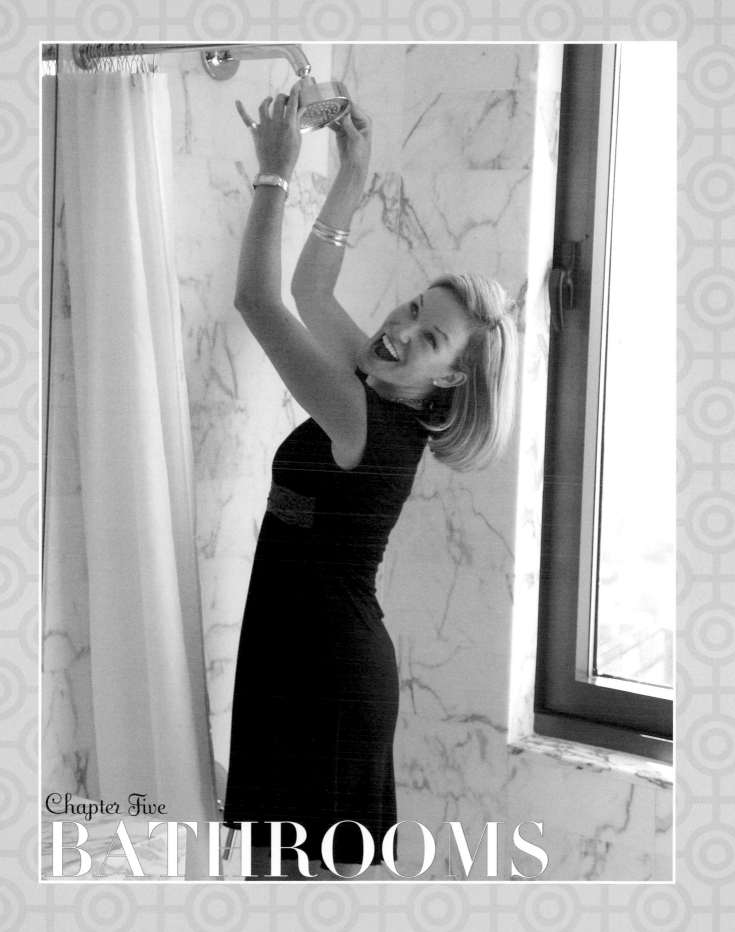

Chapter Five
BATHROOMS

In a small home, bathrooms are generally tinier than average, which leads to clutter. People tend to store tons of stuff they don't need in their bathrooms. The ensuing mess is depressing! The goal of a functional bathroom is to make it efficient for you to shower and get ready quickly and easily.

Sometimes you can splurge on luxurious building materials in a small bathroom, such as marble and tiles, because you need smaller amounts.

Creative Storage Spaces

If you have a pedestal sink and no room for toiletry storage, consider using a sink skirt. It will enable you to store toiletries under your sink, covered up by the skirt, and it will add warmth and charm to the space. They come in a variety of colors and patterns, so have some fun choosing one that enhances the design of your bathroom. If you do have a cabinet, mount the sink so it sits above the counter instead of dropping it below the counter surface to maximize that precious storage space under the vanity—this also packs a style punch!

If you have a window in your bathroom (lucky you!), hang small glass shelves in front of it to store more attractive items that you don't need to hide away, such as bath salts, soaps, and lotions. It will add valuable storage and privacy without blocking the natural light.

A full-length spice rack can store more than just seasonings. You can easily find these inexpensive racks at a home improvement store. They can help you organize cleansers, lotions, toiletries, cotton balls, deodorant, and so on. If you don't have any available wall space, mount one on the back of your bathroom door and put the open wire parts to use. You can hang hair bands or other items from hooks attached to the wire sections. In the wall space above your bathroom door, install high shelving to make use of otherwise wasted space. Just make sure to store items that you won't need to access every day.

Sink skirts can be tailored and chic—they don't have to be those floral shirred things that you'd see in your grandmother's house. They give you a place to hide toiletries and bathroom supplies.

Above-the-counter mounted sinks help free up some valuable under-the-counter space.

If you have drywall in your bathroom, you may be able to remove it, which will expose the studs. Paint the studs and mount small shelves in between them. You've now created small recessed niches that can house anything from toiletries to linens—even an ironing board! If you want to add an extra design element, consider wallpapering the backs of the niches . . . no one will ever believe you created all that additional storage just by removing some Sheetrock!

Hanging from a Hook

Bathrooms often require somewhere to hang items such as towels and robes, but if you don't have enough room for a few large towel bars, here are some alternate solutions:

- Mount a few swag holders (the ones usually reserved for holding your grandmother's swoopy drapes) in your bathroom. They hang on the wall and have a large hole in the middle and a little shelf area on top. You can hang hand towels in the opening and place candles or perfumes on the shelf. Because they are small, you can fasten them wherever you find space in your bathroom, which gives you more flexibility than the traditional towel bar.

- Use a wall-mount coatrack that has a shelf on top. You can hang towels and robes on the hooks and keep toiletries and shower supplies on the shelf.

Above: Wire racks that are usually used in a kitchen pantry work really well in a bathroom to hold all sorts of items.

Right: When you're looking for more storage space and all else fails, just look up! The area in a bathroom over the door is a perfect spot to store towels and baskets with less frequently used items.

• If finding wall space in general is challenging in your tiny bathroom, use a lean metal ladder (the type you'd use in a small library) as a towel bar. Attach hooks to the sides of the ladder to hold robes or small sacks to hold kids' bath toys.

Often the action of hanging something you wouldn't ordinarily think to hang can solve an entirely different design dilemma, such as where to find room for all of your primping products when you have limited cabinet, drawer, or linen closet space. If you find that you *do* have some wall space but don't have enough storage in general, mount a bunch of towel bars on the walls. Instead of hanging towels, though, hang S hooks to hold bathing supplies and baskets filled with soaps, lotions, and toiletries. Or install a Peg-Board on available wall space to hang small wire baskets that can store toiletries and attach hooks from which you can hang towels. You can also fill handled baskets with your bathroom essentials and hang them on the wall with cup hooks, which screw right into the wall. These hooks were originally designed to screw in under a wall cabinet in the kitchen to hold teacups, but in a small space they are invaluable. You don't need a power tool to install them—just a flick of the wrist! Finally, try using metal magazine racks to store your rolled up clean towels.

A Shower of Ideas

If you have a really tiny bathroom, you can trick the eye and visually make it appear larger by hanging your shower curtain higher. Have a longer shower curtain made, or add a 12-inch band of fabric to an existing shower curtain, and watch your little room grow! By placing it higher, it draws your eye upward, making the ceiling seem higher and the room more spacious.

Use a dual-rod shower curtain rod, which has two rods (one outer rod traditionally used for a decorative shower curtain and an inner rod for the shower curtain liner), but hang the shower curtain and the liner on the same rings on the inner rod and use the outer rod as a towel bar. You can also hang S hooks off the outer rod to hang bathrobes, bags of bath toys, and any other toiletries that can hang from a hook!

Cup hooks are great for renters—you just screw them into your walls. No drilling or tools necessary!

LIBBY'S TRICKS OF THE TRADE

Don't Break the Bank—How to Affordably Change the Look and Feel of Your Small Bathroom

Mirrored medicine cabinets are functional for storage but they also visually expand the look of a small bathroom.

- Stain your grout either black or white.

- Put mirrors on the face of the vanity cabinets and doors. This will quickly and inexpensively update your bathroom as well as visually open up the space.

- Stack standard-size mirrored medicine cabinets. They use vertical space well in a bathroom, providing storage space and reflecting light.

- Create an eye-catching towel bar by hanging a sturdy tree limb or piece of bamboo (about 1½ inch in diameter) in drapery rod supports. If the tree limb has forks

The floating glass shelf over the toilet in this bathroom is a great spot to put things, and because it's glass it keeps it feeling airy and open.

A small powder room is a chance to have some fun with wall color. This rich brown makes it feel stylish and intimate.

and other limbs shooting off of it, you can hang smaller items (such as washcloths) on them as well.

• Consider putting mirrors on an entire wall to open up the space.

• Use Japanese mats on the floor and black river rocks to hold down their sides for a change in ambience. Or tack the mats to the walls!

• Paint the wall above your shower tiles a new color.

• Buy a commercial stainless-steel organizer to mount on your wall. It will allow you the flexibility to move different shelves and storage around as you need to, and the stainless steel is a great reflective surface that looks cool and is easy to keep clean. Be sure to mix in a small plant or a few little decorative items to keep it from looking too industrial.

• Use a modern floating wall shelf for bathroom storage—it can hold everything from rolled up towels to small baskets of soap, toiletries, and toilet paper. It's called a floating shelf because there are no supports below or above it; a metal clamp is screwed into the wall and the shelf fits over the metal clamp and appears to float.

• If you don't have space on your floor for a magazine rack, mount a skinny ladder to your wall and hang magazines and newspapers over the rungs.

• Organize under-vanity space with a sliding rack that can be mounted to the inside of the vanity. You can find these units at home improvement stores. They are mostly used in kitchens, but think about all that wasted space between the underside of the counter and the bottom of the cabinet. Put that area to work!

• Hang hairbrushes and hair dryers from holsters and hooks mounted on the side of your vanity.

Fill your small bathroom with fabulous bath goodies. It can be small yet luxurious!

Chapter Six
BEDROOMS

What do people want most from their bedrooms? Usually

it's comfort, personal style, and storage. While we all often want the same things from our bedrooms, the way we use our bedrooms can truly vary. Some people want a serene, quiet space in which to wind down at the end of the day, others want to stay up in bed and watch late-night TV, and still others want a bright, cheerful spot to do a crossword on Sunday morning. There are dozens of ways to personalize your bedroom and make it function for the way you live, whether you want it to feel like a cozy sleeping space or a more open yet serene quality. I see a small bedroom as an opportunity to create a space that's all your own—a room that revives you, recharges you, and gives you a big warm hug at the end of a long day.

For me, bedrooms are among the most fun rooms to design. People are more likely to take chances with colors and patterns than they normally would in a main living space; they figure it's just a bedroom, it's more contained, and they don't spend that many waking hours there. Small bedrooms pose their own challenges both in designing a layout that maximizes the space you *do* have as well as in finding the right amount of storage for your needs. I have some great tips to get you on your way to bedroom bliss and plenty of pictures to inspire you to build a nest that's just right for the way you choose to use your room!

How to Spice Up the Bedroom

If your bedroom is lacking in the personality department (okay . . . who are we kidding, it just screams

Mixing chocolate brown with citron green looks modern and fresh, and using a white coverlet keeps it from looking too dark or busy. Notice the bold pattern is just used as an accent on the shams.

"blah!"), you can jazz it up by layering your bed linens. (For step-by-step instructions, see Libby's Tricks of the Trade: Luxurious Beds—How to Layer Your Bed Linens on page 124.) Choose a bedspread/duvet, shams, and throw pillows in a mixture of patterns and colors. This will add more depth and dimension to a small bedroom than one overstuffed comforter in a solid color. Make sure you choose subtle patterns, and don't use more than three colors at once or it will look like a circus!

High Headboards

A high headboard—at least 7 feet tall—will create the feeling of more space and greater height in your room. For a unique, personality-driven alternative to the standard headboard, use one or more old doors, or screens. You can mount them high up on the wall over your bed using L brackets, or, if you're not terribly handy with a drill, rest them on the floor (as long as they are tall) to get the same effect. Or, hang drapes floor to ceiling behind your bed—even if you have a headboard—for an elegant, cozy look. It's inexpensive and easy to do. For most rooms with standard ceiling heights, you simply need a 96-inch drapery panel

This high head-board gives the illusion of more space—and adds a very luxurious element to the room, too!

instead of the 84-inch panel . . . a simple change with strikingly different results.

Create your own dramatic headboard using plywood, a piece of foam, your favorite fabric, and a staple gun. You can make it as high as you want and any color that suits your style. Begin by having a piece of plywood or MDF board (which is lighter in weight) cut to the width of your mattress and about 62 inches high (or as high as you'd like your headboard). Your local hardware store or lumberyard can precut the wood for you (yes, there are lumberyards, even in New York City). Have them notch out the space below the bed frame, box spring, and mattress but still leave about 7 inches of width on either side to act as leg supports; notching out the space keeps it from being superheavy.

Next, buy a piece of 3-inch-thick foam the width of the headboard and the height of the front face of the headboard, from the top of the mattress to the top of the headboard. Hot glue the piece of foam to the front face of the board; this will help hold it in place when you're working on it. Choose an upholstery fabric you like (this fabric is wider than that you'd use to sew clothing; it's usually at least 54 inches wide). Cut the fabric to allow for an 8-inch border all the way around the foam. Cut two pieces of fabric large enough to fold around the two leg sections; these won't be covered in foam, but they do need to be covered in fabric so there's no exposed wood.

Spread the fabric for the foam section of the headboard out on the floor so that the right side (the side you want facing out on your headboard) faces the floor. Place the headboard on top of the fabric, the foam side facing the wrong side of the fabric and the 8-inch border sticking out evenly all the way around the headboard. Now pull the top center piece of fabric up

Even if you use a high headboard, don't be afraid to put some artwork above it; remember, any time things can go up towards the ceiling, it draws your eye upward and makes the room feel larger!

over the foam and staple it nice and tight to the backside of the board. Just put in a few staples to secure it—you'll complete it after you've secured the other four edges. Next pull the right center side of the fabric border over and staple it to the back and repeat this with the left center side and the bottom center piece. By rotating around the board, stapling only the center of each side of the fabric, you have more control of the fabric and can keep it even as you go along. Then you can start pulling and stapling the rest of the fabric about every 2 inches all the way around the board. Fold the corners nice and sharp, as if you were wrapping a present, for a clean, sleek look. Now lay out the "leg" pieces of fabric on the floor, right side down, and staple the border edges to the back of the board to cover the legs.

Stand your headboard up and place it behind your bed. With tall headboards it's sometimes better to mount them directly to the wall rather than attaching them to the back of the bed frame; this can be done by screwing the leg section of the headboard into your wall at both the bottom and top of the legs. Push your bed up in front of the headboard, admire your handy work, and get a good night's sleep!

For another creative design, turn an old fireplace mantle into a headboard. You can use the entire front face of a fireplace (vertical supports as well as the mantle) or just the top mantle section. If you use the entire fireplace, staple gun some fabric to what would have been the fireplace opening so that you don't have a gap between your mattress and box spring and the wall. If you only use the top mantle section, you can hang it as high or as low as you like over your bed. To maximize storage mount three or four floating shelves on the wall above the mantle. They can serve as a dramatic focal point in the space as well as a perfect spot to display art objects, books, and pictures. Floating shelves don't require brackets; instead they are secured by mounting a metal clamp or "cleat" to the wall, and then the shelf attaches over the clamp and hangs on the wall. It provides a more open look than a closed-in shelf—a great visual option for a small space.

Floor-to-ceiling bookcases can also be used as a headboard, and they too make a personal statement. The bookcases don't have to be custom built; you can buy them premade. Make sure that they stand as tall as possible and no more than 12 inches deep so that they'll give you tons of storage but won't devour too much square footage. Visually, a tall wall of bookshelves creates height and depth and makes a room appear much larger. If you're a book person, this is a fantastic way to focus your collection in one spot, which adds impact and gives you full credit for your library. And if you catch a bad dose of insomnia, just turn around and pick out a book!

Fun with Furniture

You can freshen up the front of an old dresser by applying some cool wallpaper to the faces of the drawers; this will make the piece an interesting focal point without having bold wallpaper (on your walls) overwhelm your small space. Paint the top of the dresser—and everything else but the drawers—a color that works with the wallpaper you've selected and you'll have a fun custom piece of furniture!

Place a skinny bench, no deeper than 14 inches—one that speaks to your personal style—at the foot of your bed. In addition to being a great spot to sit and put on your shoes, it serves as a footboard and also creates storage for magazines and books below it. You can add some warmth and texture to the room by using a fabric-covered seat cushion on top of the bench. If you don't

Libby-ism

In a small bedroom use a high headboard but skip the footboard. Footboards make a room feel smaller and take up valuable space. (And just think: You can avoid stubbing your toe—that's right, no more bumping into the footboard when you get up in the middle of the night!)

Above: I covered these drawer faces in a textured seagrass wallpaper and added new nickel drawer pulls for elegance and contrast. It's a fast update to an old piece of furniture.

Right: Even if you have a small bedroom, you may have room at the foot of your bed for a bench. You can store things under it, and a coordinating cushion cover that works with your bedding can be a nice accent.

space to incorporate a few choice, hard-working pieces of furniture.

Contrary to popular belief, armoires hog an enormous amount of space in a small bedroom, and they don't really give you that much storage in return. You're better off installing 16–inch-deep floor-to-ceiling shelves (which hold a folded shirt or sweater perfectly) and concealing them with drapes. With a hospital curtain tracking system or drapery rod, you can hang the drapes from the ceiling 17 inches from the wall. The hospital curtain tracking system is literally a track that mounts onto the ceiling, and the drapery hooks are on little rollers or wheels that slide easily within the track. The drapes extend all the way up to the ceiling, hiding the storage behind them and softening the feel of the room by adding an element of fabric. If you also need hanging space, you can begin your shelving a bit higher up the wall (about 40 inches from the floor) and mount a closet rod to the underside of the bottom shelf. This creates the perfect area for shorter hanging items such as shirts, folded slacks, and shorts.

Nightstands can also waste space. If your bedside tables lack shelves or drawers, drape them with a floor-length cloth to cover items you want to store below. I hide luggage underneath one bedside table and a basket for clothes that need to go to the dry cleaners under the other!

For additional clothes storage, substitute your nightstands with small three-drawer chests; they make your room look really luxurious and elegant and add oodles of storage for folded items. People often think they don't have enough room for two small dressers on either side of the bed, but they actually do. You can either fill up your room with

have the time or money to have a custom cushion sewn, buy a piece of 3–inch-thick foam and cut a piece of cardboard, as well as the foam, to the size of the bench top. Buy enough fabric to cover the tops and edges and to wrap around to the underside of the foam. Place the cardboard on the underside of the foam, wrap both in the fabric, and staple the fabric to the cardboard. Secure the cardboard side of your cushion to the benchtop with some carpet tape to keep it from slipping.

Small-Space Storage Solutions

Sometimes your bedroom feels like a cluttered matchbox, because you have no real storage and literally nowhere to put anything away. So rather than keep all your clothes in rotating laundry hampers, look around the room and see where you have

Notice how each of these small dressers or chests gives you more room for storage than a traditional bedside table and creates a more luxurious look as well!

tons of smaller pieces of furniture that don't really function, or you can choose fewer items that hold more to help your room feel less cluttered and maximize storage.

Another alternative to a traditional nightstand is to chop a round kitchen table in half and mount the center-cut sections to the wall on either side of your bed. All you need is a cleat support under the section that's mounted to the wall; the legs will support the outside section. You can make a skirt for the table and use the covered area below for storage. A neat extra touch would be to have two semicircle mirrors cut for the tops of the tables—it would look dressier and reflect the lamplight from your bedside lamps!

Sometimes immovable objects in your room can cause wasted space, leaving you

wondering where to fit that much-needed shelving or filing cabinet. If you have a wall-mounted air-conditioning unit, such as the long, skinny metal ones found in

Libby-ism

Use 12-inch-square mirror tiles (sold in boxes at home improvement stores) to line the tops of your walls along the ceiling to make your space feel bigger. You can also mount mirrors on the back of shelving units, which will bounce light back into your space, giving the illusion of a larger room.

The mirror faces on this small chest reflect light and visually open up the room.

lots of rental apartments, extend that same long line to reach to the walls on either side of the unit by building shallow cabinetry on either side. This creates a clean line that adds tons of storage in an otherwise wasted space, and it also makes the wall appear longer. Plus you can use the shelf area above the cabinetry to showcase framed pictures and small collectibles.

If your mattress is on a frame (and not directly on your floor) you can increase potential storage space by putting lifts under your bed, which you can find at any home improvement or bedding and bath store. When you place the lifts under the legs of your bed frame, you can literally "lift" your

bed about 7 inches off the floor. The standard "drop," or length of a bed skirt, is 15 inches, but you can buy an extra-long bed skirt at 21 inches to compensate for your exciting new height. (It sounds crazy, but it really is thrilling when you see how much storage space you gain.) With all that space you can store your less-used/seasonal items—or additional sheet sets—in bins underneath your bed. Buy long, skinny storage bins with wheels, which are specifically designed for use under beds (the wheels make them super easy to access). Choose clear bins so that you can easily

identify what's in them. You can also tack hanging shoe-storage organizers so that they fall down the side of your dust skirt (over your box spring), and use them to stash remote controls, magazines, and bedside reading.

Closet Space

Sometimes simple changes can give the impression that you have more space. If you have space-sucking closet doors, take them off and replace them with curtains that reach up to the ceiling along a hospital

Above left: A simple hanging shoe organizer works well over a bed skirt as a spot to hold bedside items that might take up valuable space on your nightstand.

Above right: This big basket slides underneath your bedside table and is the perfect place to stash laundry or dry cleaning; if you have multiple bins, you can use tags to identify what's in them for easy access.

Right: Using hospital track mounted on the ceiling enables you to cover the entire closet opening from floor to ceiling so it looks more like a wall of fabric instead of a closet.

Right: The door was removed from this closet and replaced with a curtain that is mounted on the ceiling. A standard-size closet can turn into a recessed storage/entertainment area that allows you to put a small dresser in the bottom as well as a television, books, and baskets on shelving.

The mirrored face of this bedside cabinet is super chic. And it bounces the natural light around the room.

curtain tracking system. Your eyes will be drawn up to the ceiling, creating an illusion of more height. You'll also truly add more space, because you won't need to allow for the door clearance when it opens into your room, and the new curtains slide from side-to-side.

You can put a media station into a closet as well. When you want your bedroom to feel cozier, the curtains can hide the system. Look at the curtain fabric as an opportunity to add some style to the room, whether you choose a color or great texture. Just be sure to steer clear of really

Adding mirrors to inset panels of existing closet doors is a great way to update the look of what you already have as well as visually open up the space and reflect natural light.

big, bold patterns that can visually clutter your room, making it feel smaller.

You can also update the look of existing closets—or cabinets—by covering the faces of the doors with mirrors. This will visually open up the space as well as add some style to what you already have. Most mirror companies will come to your home to measure, cut the mirror, and install it pretty inexpensively.

If you have a really tiny closet with one small door, consider adding Peg-Board to the back of the door to organize belts, small purses, hats, or necklaces.

In a bedroom you can have some fun with color; this bright green is great but it's broken up with artwork over the headboard and mixed with crisp black and white.

Choosing Colors Carefully

Sometimes people tell me they want color in their bedrooms, but they fear that if they paint their walls, the room will look even smaller. Color has the power to dramatically change the feeling of a room—it can change its character or ambience with a stroke of a brush.

Color choices should be based on the mood you want to create in your space. Light colors evoke a sense of serenity, while dark colors make a room feel like a haven. Color is a personal choice. Look at things that make you feel at peace and rested and base your wall color on

that. Do not let fear dissuade you from try-ing something new. Trust your instincts and go with your gut (and when all else fails, find a picture of a bedroom in a magazine that you'd love to live in and try to recreate it).

Some people like the softness and energy of a soft, pale color, while others enjoy the warm, snuggly feeling of a rich, dark hue. Keep in mind that you can bal-ance a dark wall color with a headboard that contrasts with the wall—whether through paint, fabric, or wallpaper. You can also balance a bold wall color in a small room with large artwork that breaks it up and adds visual interest. Also, don't be afraid to experiment. Remember: You can paint an accent wall behind your bed, and if you don't like it, or you grow tired of it, it's

easy enough to change it when you're ready for a new look . . . have some fun!

You can also incorporate a bold wall color by painting what I call a "frame area" around your headboard, a piece of artwork, or a hat collection . . . anything on your wall that can serve as a focal point in your room. Simply paint a solid box in a bold color around the object. For example, if you have three 16 x 20 inch framed pictures that you plan to arrange on your wall, decide where you want to place them and then paint three 20 x 24 inch boxes on the wall in a rich color that will highlight the frames. Then hang the pictures inside the boxes, leaving an even amount of color all the way around them, and you've introduced some bold color without taking over your entire room!

Left: The pale blue wall color creates a soothing, tranquil atmosphere in this room.

Above: The large mirror placed next to the bed opens up the space and makes it feel much more expansive.

The dark navy wall color in this bedroom creates the feeling of a snuggly little haven, but it's broken up with a high headboard and artwork with bright white mattes hung above it.

Here I've painted a dark navy box on the wall to highlight the artwork over the bed. White frames are a great contrast and make the items pop. See how the navy frame behind the bed accentuates the artwork, creating a more dramatic backdrop. Asymmetrically hung artwork makes the wall visually interesting and makes for a livelier look.

Libby's before and afters:

Before: The window shades mounted just above the windows don't add any softness; they feel cold and stark.

After: The floor-to-ceiling drapes create more height in this room, and they soften the harsh lines of the window frames. The comfy chair and ottoman provide a cozier sitting area, and the upholstered bench with storage inside replaces a traditional footboard.

Libby's before and afters:

Before: This room had no personality—white walls and stark blinds don't help, and the bare floor is not inviting at all.

After: The first thing I did was paint the walls a soft color that would add some contrast with the white molding and shutters. This room now has a more sophisticated look, and even with the additional furniture, it looks larger! It looks more like a welcoming bedroom than just a place to crash at night.

LIBBY'S TRICKS OF THE TRADE

Luxurious Beds—How to Layer Your Bed Linens for a Luxe Look (What it means to "layer" and why you really need to do it!)

We want our bedroom to feel like a retreat or getaway—it should be a place that beckons us to take a load off, rest, and recharge. One of the biggest mistakes I see in bedrooms has to do with bed linens and how people actually make their beds. We all grow up as kids hearing, "Don't forget to make your bed," and for many of us it's a chore that we still fight every step of the way. But what some of us don't realize is that with a little more effort, and maybe another blanket and a few more pillows, we can instantly and inexpensively transform the entire look and feel of our bedroom.

I often hear from clients, "I see those beds in magazines and catalogs, but I can never get mine to look like that. It's always a rumpled mess with limp pillows, but I don't have all day to starch and press my bedding." I reply, "Good grief, even if you had that kind of time, is that how you'd really want to spend it, starching and pressing bed linens?" More than likely the answer is no. So here's the skinny on how to take your bed from ho-hum to heavenly:

Because of the strong pattern of the wallpaper, the best choice was to keep the bedding clean and simple, incorporating the blue and tan of the wallpaper on a predominantly white background.

Use multiple elements

• **Duvet:** This is a big, soft "sheet envelope" that you put a down comforter inside. Duvets come in a whole range of colors and patterns; you may want to find one with a pattern, because you will fold it into quarters and set it at the foot of your bed. This will keep the pattern from overwhelming your small space, and with the comforter inside it adds nice height at the foot of your bed.

• **Blanket or coverlet:** A coverlet is a thin quilt-like blanket that rests on top of your sheet and tucks into the space between the box spring and mattress. Use a solid one without a pattern. If you want a less-expensive version, a nice, thick woven cotton blanket will give you the same result.

• **Bed skirt or dust ruffle:** This is a decorative covering that you place under a mattress and let it hang to the floor (concealing any under-the-bed storage). Don't be afraid of a "bed skirt." This isn't that flowery, ruffled thing that your grandmother has on the beds in her house . . . you're too cool for that. Bed skirts come in all colors and sizes. The sleeker version is the straight "box pleat" bed skirt—it has clean lines and hides the space between your bed frame and mattress while adding another layer below your bed. I have a special trick that I use with bed skirts: I look at the finish on the floor, and if it's dark wood or dark carpeting, then I use a light bed skirt, and if the floor is light, I use a darker bed skirt. This contrast adds visual interest.

Notice how the dark bed skirt contrasts with the beige rug.

This patterned sham helps conceal the pillow behind it and really pops in front of the bright red headboard.

- **Sheets:** This layer is self-explanatory, but it's a chance to add some pattern if you want to because, as with the duvet, only a small amount will show, and it won't overpower or visually clutter the feeling of space in your room.

- **Shams:** These are covers used over fluffy pillows, mostly for display. Shams are the unsung heroes of your bed—they look great, work hard, and give you that "ah" factor. Begin in the back by placing your sleeping pillows closest to the wall or headboard; you don't really want to see them, and this is the perfect place to hide them. Then start with the tallest shams—the Euro shams. These are 26-inch square, they add height, and they are a great anchor to your bed whether you have a headboard or not. For a queen-size bed, two Euro shams work well. If you want patterned shams, let these have the pattern, because you'll just get a hint of it from behind the other pillows. In front of the Euro shams, place two standard shams (they will be lower than the Euros) in a softer pattern or a solid. These shams start to "build out" the look of your bed and give it that super comfy feel. If you want to incorporate some decorative pillows, you can place them in front of the standard shams for a super luxurious look. If you

find some fantastic throw pillows that you adore but would normally be used on a sofa, don't be afraid to put them in the bedroom—a pillow you love is a pillow you love no matter what room it winds up in!

You now have seven layers from the bottom up

1. **The floor:** Try to contrast your bed skirt with the floor.

2. **The bed skirt:** Depending on your style, it can be frilly or streamlined.

3. **The coverlet/blanket:** This is usually better as a solid, since it's what you'll see the most of, but look for cool quilted patterns or stitch work to keep it interesting.

4. **The duvet:** This can be solid or patterned and will add visual interest if it contrasts with the bed skirt. Keep it stuffed with a comfy comforter and folded at the foot of the bed.

5. **The sheets:** These are an important layer; fold back the top sheet over the coverlet/blanket to add more dimension.

6. **The shams:** These give height to your bed as well as depth. They can also keep it interesting when you layer a few of them in multiple fabrics.

7. **Decorative accent pillows:** These act as the cherry on top and work well if you're going for a glamorous look.

Maintenance tips

- Don't ever wash your duvet cover or shams. Have them dry-cleaned periodically; this will keep them looking crisp and sharp rather than limp and wilted.

- Consider getting a fluffy mattress topper (especially if you don't have a pillow-top mattress), which goes over the mattress and under the sheets (these are often made of memory foam). Upscale hotels use mattress toppers to lure customers back. They're super cushy and make for a very soft night's sleep.

- Buy sturdy, thick pillow fillers for your shams, no matter how expensive (or inexpensive) your bedding is. None of it looks good with wimpy, flat pillows.

- You don't have to spend loads of money on bedding—so many discount stores (TJ Maxx, Marshalls, Target, HomeGoods) have fabulous-looking bedding that you can mix and match.

- Don't buy bedding in sets or all in one bag; it will look one dimensional and like a "bed blob." Break it up and layer different sheets with blankets and shams. To keep it looking cohesive and not too cluttered with color, work with no more than three colors at a time. For example, white, aqua, and chocolate brown—a cream rug, chocolate bed skirt, white/aqua/chocolate duvet, chocolate Euro shams, and white and aqua shams. Each piece is different, but they work together for a focused, elegant look.

- Think of yourself as a bed builder: You're the architect, and you're creating an inviting boudoir you'll want to run and jump into!

Winter Stuff

Chapter Seven
HOME OFFICES

Ah, the good old home office . . . Years ago people left their offices and actually went home—now we all seem to have to have a home office! Not only do we need a work space, we need space for all our technology: computers, printers, scanners, faxes, and paper shredders. It's a lot to navigate even in a large space, but in a tiny space you really need to have your game plan focused and functional.

Sometimes you can eke out a work space in an underutilized corner in your living room—often corner spaces are wasted!

In small homes it's rare to have an entire room designated solely as an office. So the space you create needs to be accessible, efficient, and organized. Often it has to serve double duty. Lighting and storage options are key; you don't want your space to feel even more confining because it's dark or cluttered. I'm not in the business of helping to create workaholics, but I figure if you need to incorporate a work space in your home, why not find a way to make it look great?

I will show you how to seamlessly blend your home office into your home environment so that you can get things accomplished but don't feel as if you're sleeping at your job when you turn off your light at night! I have some terrific ideas to help you get your small home office space running like a well-oiled machine!

A Double-Duty Office Space

If you don't have a separate room to designate as an office, there are ways to lay out another room so that the office doesn't take over the entire space. The first step is to divide it creatively! In partitioning spaces, don't be afraid to float your bookcases in the middle of the room.

You can also put bookshelves on tracks or rolling casters and allow them to function as mobile room dividers. Just don't fill them too full of books or you'll create a dark barrier that screams "space divider!" You

Above: Here is the hospital track system that mounts from the ceiling and allows the fabric to reach all the way up.

Above: The track has two wheels set inside, and the curtains are attached with grommets so it's super easy to pull the curtains from side to side.

Left: Here you can see the office storage system that has been set up behind the curtain. Lots of file baskets, bags, and bins are mobile enough to pull out when you need to work on something and then can slip back into their designated spot when they are not needed.

Above: The glass table doubles as a work space by day but a dining table by night, and because it's glass it visually keeps it airy and open in the tight space. You can see that when the curtains are closed they really just act as a soft wall of fabric and allow you to tuck your work away for the night.

Above: I turned a double closet in a bedroom into an office space; there's just enough room for a desk and shelving for office supplies.

Right: You don't want to waste an inch of vertical space; the bins above are great for storage and the ribbon fabric board is a great place to stow smaller items you need or want to keep handy.

Far right: This is me with my grandmother, and the stool and desk I used here are family heirlooms from her.

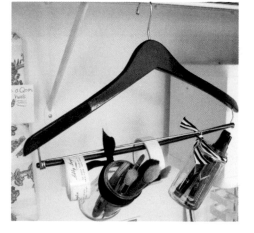

Far left: These wire baskets are fantastic because they instantly attach over any existing wire shelving; no drilling or nailing necessary.

Left: This is a simple wooden coat hanger with some pickle jars attached by ribbon. See what you already have lying around your house that you might be able to put to work!

still want light and air to pass through, plus packed rolling shelves are too heavy to move. If you need more privacy, consider frosted glass to back the open shelving in on one side. It will give you the privacy you need yet still allow natural light to pass through. While your office can be on one side of the bookcases, you can have a bench or a loveseat back up to the other side as delineation for your living room.

An old glass-paned door can also act as a good room divider—it will let light through the glass panes but still give you a sense of separation. You can mount it perpendicularly on a wall with L brackets and secure it at the bottom with a 2 x 4 (you can paint or stain the 2 x 4 to match the color of the door or the floor).

You can also create a home office out of a double closet. I bet that's not the space you were thinking of transforming! A standard double closet's dimensions are 70 inches wide by 24 inches deep. This allows room for a workstation, file drawers, storage shelves, and a computer or TV. Add lighting with a lamp to brighten it up and use a stool that can be pushed completely under the desk so that when you're not working you can close the doors and forget about work for a while.

Another thing you can do is put a desk in a hallway—if the hallway is 4½ feet wide. In fact, a built-in desk, 36 inches wide by 19 inches deep, can turn a corridor into a functional work space. Mount shallow 12-inch wall-hung shelves above the desk to utilize the vertical space. Or use a shelf *as your desk* by installing an 18-inch-deep shelf 30 inches up from the floor. Just be sure to carve out a little hole on the side that's against the wall to feed computer and electric cords through.

For an office/dining room combination, use a stainless-steel worktable as both your desk and dining table. They come with large locking wheels and can be found at most restaurant-supply stores, and often they have a bonus storage shelf or drawer below the work surface.

Illuminating and Enlarging Your Work Space

You need substantial lighting in an office, but it can be hard to find room on your desktop with all of the equipment and supplies you need. Instead of opting for the traditional desk lamp, install a wall sconce lamp, add a floor lamp, or aim a wall-mounted spotlight at the corner angles to open it up. (Corners tend to be darker than the rest of a room.) Remember: If

If your desk is very small, a skinny buffet lamp might be a better choice than a standard wider table lamp—it will keep your work space more open.

Left: If you are really lacking in the desktop space department, consider mounting a good, bright wall sconce next to your desk; it will give off light but not hog your desktop area.

Right: A swing arm lamp is a fabulous choice to go next to a desk, because not only is it not taking up valuable work space but you can move it where you need the light.

you can't see it in the space, it's as if it's not there—thus closing in the size of your room. Part of the secret to making your work space feel larger means finding and creating unique sources of light.

In a small office space, it's a good idea to use pieces made of stainless steel and glass. These surfaces reflect light, which will enlarge the look of the space as well as add to a cleaner look. They are easy to maintain, and often you can find a cool, unexpected piece to convert into an interesting desk simply by adding a slab of glass on top. I've found extraordinary things at flea markets, yard sales, and online auctions. Sometimes you have to be a little more patient with this route, but the savings can make it worth the wait. Shops or restaurants going out of business can provide another outlet for finding some cool, cheap home office items. Check your local paper regularly for announcements; sometimes they simply want someone to come and pick up the items so that they don't have to dispose of them. (How cool would it be to have a

chopping block from an old pizzeria as your desk?)

Think outside the box and you'll be surprised at how much is out there for the taking. Try anything from an old piece of wrought-iron gate to an antique door in a dimension roughly 30 inches wide by 56 inches long (or any size that will fit in your designated desk area). Look at ordinary items in a new way and let your imagination run wild. You can simply flip a piece on its side, get some steel industrial workhorse legs as the base supports, and have a piece of glass cut to fit the top. You'll have an inexpensive yet inspiring work space, and the glass will furnish you with a smooth work surface no matter what salvaged piece you use!

To create a greater sense of depth, and to reflect the daylight or evening light that you have in the room, mount mirrors on the backs of bookcases or shelves. Just don't overstuff the shelves with books and big items; you want to keep them a little open so the mirrors can add to the feeling of more space.

If you plan to use wood paneling on your walls, be sure it's a light wood or pale finish. Dark wood paneling can close in on a small room and make it feel cramped, plus the look can be a bit dated.

Often you have storage but it can't be dedicated to just storing one type of item. Here you see there's everything from a TV and fax to clear bins holding clothing and accessories. Just jump in and work with what you've got. Because this storage goes all the way up to the ceiling, it's a great use of vertical space!

{Sharp-looking Shelving}

Shelves are integral to work spaces, especially in smaller offices. Here are some tips for how to use them to organize your space:

- When installing shelves, measure the items you plan to store there and then hang the shelves accordingly. You don't want to lose an inch of space.

- A wall of storage doesn't have to be custom built; you can buy premade units and stack them on top of each other. Just make sure to fasten them securely to the wall! As with all other items, the higher up they go towards the ceiling, the more dramatic the effect.

- To add visual interest to a wall of shelves or add some punch to plain old metal shelving units, paint or wallpaper the inside back wall. This will give you a shot of color, accentuate the items you display, and make the shelving seem like a much more substantial piece.

- Dedicate an entire wall to house your library; it will look more focused and feel less cluttered than scattering books all over the room.

- Create a sky-high library by mounting 1-inch-thick by 9-inch-deep boards on the wall about 12 inches down from the ceiling; the length will depend on the length of your wall. Use sturdy bracket supports and place all sorts of infrequently used smaller items on the shelves as well as small-scale books you've already read. Keep it looking open by attaching mirror strips on the underside of the boards, which will reflect light from the room and make it feel much more airy.

- Instead of your typical shelves, mount clear Plexiglas mail holders all along one wall. They can hold much more than just mail, and visually, because of their clear consistency, they look less bulky than plastic or metal ones and won't close in your small space. For some additional fun, line the inside of the mail holder, which faces out, with family pictures, kids' artwork, vacation shots, or anything you think will brighten up your office!

- Mount a ready-to-assemble closet cubby shoe organizer to the wall up above your desk. Fill it with jars and canisters stocked with your office supplies, mail, computer disks, and so on.

- Shelving can also come in handy if you have a laundry room. Hang a shelf that spans from wall to wall over a washer and dryer in a small laundry room and mount a hanging bar below the shelf. You'll gain extra storage with the shelf as well as hanging space when you've got a batch of clean clothes!

Inventive Ideas for Your Office

Convert a bookcase into a double-sided workstation by placing the shelving perpendicular to your wall. Then chop a small table in half, cut off the legs, and mount the table halves up against the front and back sides of the bookcase. Fill the side of the bookcase that has shelves with office supplies, books, and mementos, and use the shelves below the table for additional storage. On the other side of the bookcase, mount a corkboard in the area above the table, or create a craft station and hang paper, ribbon, and craft items on shallow shelves above the table. On the sides of the bookcase, hang mail storage containers to hold frequently used files and mail.

A poultry feeder (a device that chickens peck their heads into to get seed) mounted to the wall can also serve as a unique and interesting place to sort mail. You can find them at a farm-supply store or an online source. Because it's made out of metal, it attracts magnets. Try using small screw-top jars with magnets attached to the lids below it to hold small office supplies, such as tacks, rubber bands, and paper clips.

Create a flexible storage system by covering the side of a shelving unit or a small section of wall with Peg-Board. Outfit it with lots of wire bins in varying sizes; you'll be shocked at how much space you'll gain by utilizing a normally unused area.

For items that won't easily fit in files, buy an adjustable shelving unit and purchase several extra shelves for it. Place the shelves in the unit, allowing for just enough height to fit short wire letter baskets. Label several wire baskets, place them on the shelves, and fill them with items you need

to access frequently. I do this with fabric swatches, paint chips, and carpet and wood samples that I need to retrieve regularly!

Chic Unique Storage

If you want the storage items in your home office to look less utilitarian and more attractive, consider using a variety of storage boxes. You no longer have to rely on those big, ugly plastic things. You can now choose from a huge variety of chic storage

These screw-top jars have magnetic tops and can easily hang from metal shelving or a metal strip mounted under wooden cabinets.

Below: If you're going to see your storage out in the open, make sure it's something you are going to want to look at. This designer chose some wonderful old hatboxes for items she doesn't need to regularly access.

fabric to achieve an overall organized and more elegant feel.

Peruse local thrift shops or salvage yards for commercial storage units such as architects' drafting storage cabinets, medical cabinets, school lockers, or restaurant serving-station units; these generally inexpensive alternatives to custom built-ins have a hip, industrial look. You can often find them for a steal at foreclosure auctions or going-out-of-business sales.

Create a versatile storage system by using common slat board mounted to the wall. Slat board is sold in sheets at home improvement stores and has slats that hold shelving supports, storage bins, and wire hooks and baskets. It usually comes in a bright white factory finish, but you can always paint it to match your decor. Get your wall working for you!

boxes covered in everything from beautiful fabrics to hip patterned wallpaper.

For a cheaper, crafty alternative, find paper or fabric you like and decorate your own boxes. Shoe boxes work really well—their size fits into many standard shelving units, and they are free! Use consistent color and

Declutter Your Desk

Organizing your desk is easy and elegant when you group an assortment of small attractive containers filled with paper clips, rubber bands, pens, and office supplies on top of a long, narrow rectangular tray (like the ones designed to go on the tank of your toilet in the bathroom). The tray will not only look great, it will also designate an easily accessible space for your most-often-used items.

Eggcups can provide a uniform way to organize small items on your desk or countertop; they look fabulous in all the same style, or you can mix them up for a more eclectic look! They are an old-fashioned item that you find in all sorts of shapes and colors at thrift stores, yard sales, and flea markets, and newer ones are available at cooking stores.

You can also be incredibly resourceful with how you use your desk. Hang slim office items like rulers, scissors, and head-phones from hooks attached to desk legs or sides of desks and file cabinets. Or, attach magazine holders to the sides of your desk for files you use frequently.

When deciding where to place your desk, think three-dimensional. Look around your space and instead of shoving your desk up against a wall, allow it to function as a divider and float it out into the middle of the space. This allows you to save the walls for valuable floor-to-ceiling storage units and shelving. You may find that a corner desk will suit your space better than any other spot against a wall. The bottom line is: Keep an open mind when looking for your best layout and desk placement.

If you want to completely hide your desk and tuck it away at the end of the day, hang a curved shower rod over your desk. Use two shower curtains and open them while you're working. At the end of the day, with a flick of the wrist, pull the curtains closed and no more work area! You can sew some pockets on the shower curtains to hold lightweight office supplies like mailing labels, correction fluid, and markers.

For an ingenious storage solution, make a mobile stool by attaching four casters to the bottom of a low cubby storage unit (about 20 inches high) and placing a small cushion on top. You can use the stool to sit on as well as hold items. When you aren't using it, you can stash it all the way under your desk.

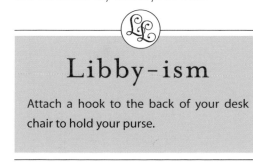

Libby-ism

Attach a hook to the back of your desk chair to hold your purse.

Rather than this desk being pushed up against a wall it's floating out in the room which feels airy and is a great use of the floor space.

You can also store supplies in a large, multibottle wine bucket with bottle brackets. Place glasses in the bottle brackets to hold pens, markers, paper clips, and tacks. Set mail and bills that need to be paid in the center section and stamps and stationary on the side sections. When you're ready to entertain, chuck everything into a box and fill the bucket with ice, a bottle of white wine, a bottle of vodka, and reserve one bracket to hold a glass of crudités and another to hold a container of dip and, voilà, you have an instant office party!

Clean Your Space and Clear Your Mind
—How to Declutter Your Home

Before I begin any makeover or redesign of a space, I make sure I throw away unnecessary items. I recommend to all my clients that they eliminate whatever they can before we get started. It's something no one wants to hear, but everyone must do! No one feels good surrounded by tons of stuff—it makes us feel confused, cramped, and overwhelmed. Most of my clients have a desire to simplify their lives, get back to basics, and live with less. And less doesn't mean without luxury. Living with less "stuff" is the ultimate luxury; people want style, elegance, and comfort, and they're realizing that this begins in a clean, organized space.

Clutter prevents you from seeing things clearly; it takes up mental and physical space. Clutter equals junk; it halts movement and progress and keeps you from being efficient and effective. Getting rid of clutter isn't about cleaning, it's about overcoming obstacles. A good decluttering session can encourage you to look at your home in an entirely new way. Everyone I know feels like a million bucks after cleaning out a closet or organizing a desk; an uncluttered space gives you the feeling that you are completely in control—you're running your home, your home isn't running you. When your space seems manageable and contained, it's bound to manifest itself in other areas of your life.

Clutter comes in different forms: It can be items that are in the wrong place, things you don't need, unfinished being nothing. What number would you prefer to represent your things? Eight? Five? If five seems about right, then your goal should be to eliminate half of your belongings. This is a process—it doesn't happen all in one day or one week. It occurs little by little, and before you know it you're coming out from under all the stuff that's been crowding your home as well as your mind!

Libby's Game Plan: Ten Steps to Clearing Clutter

1. Decide which room poses your biggest dilemma and begin there: a closet, home office, pantry, bedroom, or bathroom. This will help you remain focused and see progress in a shorter time (which will inspire you to keep going).

2. Start small, set a timer for an hour, put on some great music, light a scented candle, and know that when the timer goes off you can stop until your next session or keep going if you're feeling inspired. (Ninety-five percent of people continue, because it feels so good to start getting rid of things they don't need.)

3. Designate one garbage bag a "donate" bag and one a "pitch" bag. Toss out items that you don't need, are broken, or you haven't used. Donate clothing you haven't worn in two years, or items someone can use. Don't allow yourself to be tempted to go back into the "donate" bag and pull items out—be ruthless about what you'll keep. Shred old office documents and papers and recycle them.

4. Take your "pitch" bags out to the garbage and your "donate" bags to a nearby thrift shop or Salvation Army. Get them out of your house ASAP. Now you're starting to get there . . . just remember that organizing is a process and not a one-time event.

5. Decide which items you want to keep. But if you're saving them only to toss later, purge the clutter now. Save pictures—not objects; take a picture of your son in his scout uniform, keep the photo, and get rid of the uniform. It's the memory you're trying to hold onto, not the uniform.

The key is once you've decided to get rid of stuff, get it out of your space as soon as possible. You don't want to run the risk of going back through the bags and keeping things you've already decided you can live without!

objects left out, or belongings you haven't made a decision about yet. You need to identify the nature of your clutter, gain some perspective, and start to eliminate it.

A great way to get into the mindset of discarding or donating your things is to ask yourself, "If I had twenty minutes to evacuate my home, what would I take?" If this sounds too drastic, you can always pretend you are moving and think about items you wouldn't move (or pay someone to pack and move) into your new home. This exercise will help you to see the decluttering process as an opportunity rather than a chore. Think about how much "stuff" you are currently living with, on a scale of zero to ten—with ten being everything you own now and zero

6. Find a home for the remaining items. Everything should have a place, but not every place should have a thing. Leave some open space on shelves, countertops, and tabletops; it will keep your space feeling organized. Focus knickknacks and collections in one area instead of all over the room.

7. Be diligent about putting things back in their "home." It's faster to put things away, and it makes it easier to find them later. Avoid falling into the trap of "I'll leave it out so I remember" and "I'll stash it here for now." These rationalizations helped create your clutter.

8. Decide how much storage you need and know when it's time to add more, that usually means that it's time to eliminate items instead. Chic storage boxes consistent in color and fabric create an organized look. Measure boxes and then hang shelves that height; you don't want to waste an inch of space!

9. Live by the "In-and-Out Rule": For every item you bring home, you need to toss, recycle, or give away one item. If you receive two new sweaters for your birthday, get rid of two old sweaters.

10. Create an emergency clutter holder in a high-traffic area like the kitchen or entry area to keep mail and small essentials from cluttering countertops and passageways. Empty the holder regularly.

Decluttering your life is a powerful experience, and it's also contagious. Once you get started, you'll want to keep going. My mother always said, "You eat the elephant one bite at a time." Try not to get overwhelmed. Take it one step at a time and give yourself a pat on the back for taking charge and getting clutter, as well as your home, under control.

Chapter Eight
HALLWAYS

Hallways are often dark, closed in, and narrow and have a lot of wasted space. We frequently make the mistake of assuming that there's really not much we can do with our hallways, so we don't even try. But there are a number of ways to lighten them up, give them a more expansive feel, and use that seemingly useless space more efficiently.

Change a Dark Hallway into a Dramatic One

If your entry hall in your house feels like a dark tunnel, replace your solid-wood doors with full-length glass-paned doors. To let in light from other rooms, consider frosted glass doors or transoms. Make sure you have some sort of artificial light source, too. Track lighting, for example, looks terrific in the smallest of hallways, and you can hang pictures or artwork and angle the lights so they both highlight what's on the wall and brighten the space. You'll feel as though you're walking into your own little gallery that has depth and drama instead of your depressingly dark hallway! Track lighting lends itself to the shape of a hall, because it's long and narrow—plus it's inexpensive and readily available at most home improvement stores.

You can also replace solid-wood exterior doors with multipane and/or frosted glass doors. These doors allow in so much natural light that within a matter of hours you'll completely transform the initial feeling you have when you walk into your home. This is only an option for folks living in a home rather than an apartment, as most apartment building codes require a fireproof (therefore solid) door. But have no fear, apartment dwellers, I have lots more ideas for you!

Use silver leaf or silver paint on the ceiling; it reflects light—especially in a dark entry hall. Mirrored tiles also serve as a great choice for a hall ceiling; they make the ceiling feel higher and your hallway seem larger.

If you have dark wood floors, use a light-colored runner made of indoor/outdoor carpeting (or industrial strength). See Libby's Greatest Color Hits on page 154 for wood and paint combinations that can brighten up your space. If your hallway floors are in really bad shape, but you're not in the position to sand them or install new ones, paint them! Heavy-duty deck enamel will wear really well, and if you use a runner rug on top, you'll see only the edge of the floor for a little punch of paint. White floors can make a small space seem larger, and black high-gloss floors are dramatic. You can get really daring and paint horizontal diamonds on the floor, which will visually extend the appearance of a tiny hall.

Another way to make a design statement in a hallway is to use a ready-made indoor carpet runner; they come in a standard size—2 feet 9 inches wide by 5 feet long—and a variety of fun colors and patterns. A small hallway affords the perfect place to try a bold rug if you're so inclined. Because it's not a large area, a bright color won't make it feel any smaller—instead, it offers a quick hit of style! If you want to completely replace your flooring, a light stone or terrazzo floor gives a nice sheen and light bounces right off of it. It can make

Above: I Xeroxed black-and-white pictures on a color Xerox machine, framed them in all different sized frames, and created a gallery-type feel in this hallway. Because of the consistency of the black-and-white images and the white mattes, it looks pulled together and focused rather than cluttered.

Above: This track lighting is inexpensive and available at home improvement stores. The halogen bulbs and glass casings give it more of a high-style look than those traditional metal cans from older track lighting sets.

Right: You don't have to spend a lot of money on frames; just make sure they are as big as you can get them and that the mattes are large. They will help add height and scale to a small hallway and make it feel grander!

Above: This diagonal pattern on the carpeting would make a fabulous runner in a small hall because visually the diamonds pull your eye from one corner to the next and make it seem larger.

Above: This diagonal patterned carpeting would work well in a hallway because it is light enough to keep the space feeling open, but it's still enough of a tan color so it would wear well and not show too much dirt.

a small hallway feel much more expansive. And if you decide to use square tiles, get them as large as possible, 12-inch or 16-inch squares, and install them on the diagonal. The diagonal pattern makes the floor space appear so much longer than the standard straight-on pattern does, and it will make the hallway feel larger overall.

If you have a wall at the end of a small hallway, hang the largest mirror possible and place a bench below it. This will anchor your entryway and make it feel more important; the mirror will reflect light and brighten it up, and the bench will provide an ideal spot to set bags, mail, and magazines when you enter or put on shoes before you leave.

You can also hang shelves, floor to ceiling, at the end of a hallway to house all your books. This makes for a focused, clean-looking wall. Then use track lighting to brighten up the space and aim spotlights on your "intimate library."

Navigating a Narrow Hallway

If your hallway is long but too narrow to fit a table, you can create the feeling of a proper entryway by hanging a mirror and placing a low, shallow shelf made of crown molding underneath it. Use the shelf to place keys, loose change, and so on. The mirror will create the illusion of a greater space and the molding shelf will give you the functionality you need. Or instead of a molding shelf, mount a magnetic strip on the wall and use powerful magnets to hang keys, notes, receipts, pictures, and cards.

For additional storage, hang a grouping of old wall-mount mailboxes on the wall to organize incoming/outgoing mail as well as keep kids' school papers and keys handy. You can hang your keys, hats, scarves, and mittens on the bottom hooks that used to be reserved for holding the newspaper. Paint them all the same shade or perk up the space and paint each one a different bright color. You can usually find these mailboxes at yard sales or on eBay.

Line the walls of a small entryway or hallway with 4-inch-deep picture ledges and paint the walls behind them a bold, bright color. This is a great way to focus a collection of photographs or small collectibles without cluttering up your home. It will feel like your own personal gallery.

{Quick and Easy Ideas to Organize Your Entryway}

Here are some quick tips to get your entryway organized:

- If you have a garage, add Peg-Board on a wall close to the house entry. Hang everything from tools, sports gear, extension cords, and picnic chairs from S hooks.

- Nail a long piece of wood about 1 inch thick by 5 inches wide down one wall of your entryway and cover it with hooks of all different sizes. This is a great place to store bags, keys, coats, scarves, and accessories. It will keep them off the floor, and you'll know where everything is when it's time to go back out!

A double rod towel bar can act as the perfect place to hang regularly used items in your hallway.

S hooks allow you to hang all sorts of items from purses and backpacks to jackets and hats from the towel bar.

- Create a clutter-buster entry system. Place two long towel bars along the wall about 4 feet off the floor and two more about 6 feet off the floor. Hang large S hooks off the lower towel bars to hold backpacks, kids' coats, dog leashes, or just about anything else. Hang storage shelves and bins off the upper towel bars with S hooks and use them to store keys, books, and mail. Affix corkboard tiles or a magnetic chalkboard to the wall area in between or above the towel bars for tacking notes, reminders, and memos.

Create a central spot where everything has a place—mail, keys, and bags. You'll save tons of time by knowing right where everything is, and it doesn't create clutter throughout the rest of your space.

- Mount a row of clipboards (they come in cool colors) along the wall in your hallway. On the bottom of each clipboard, screw in coat hooks so they go through the clipboard and into the wall. You can clip memos, outgoing mail, and reminders under the metal clasp part of the clipboard and hang bags and jackets from the coat hooks below.

Clipboards are great when mounted up on your wall; they can hold everything from to-do lists, receipts, invitations, tickets, and mail.

- Fasten a kitchen utensil rail/pot rack on the inside of a hallway door to add hanging space for bags, gloves, and hats.

- You can make a simple and functional coatrack plaque for your entryway from five wooden coat hangers and a piece of wood 30 inches long by 4 inches high. Make a straight cut off one of the arms of each wooden hanger, turn the hanger upside down so the metal hook (that normally goes over the closet rod) is now inverted and becomes a hook to hang bags or keys on, and use the one wooden arm that's left (facing up toward the ceiling) to rest a hat or scarf. Attach the hangers to the board by screwing them in from behind and then mount the board on the wall.

Simple cup hooks screwed into the bottom of the clipboards can hold keys, the dog leash, or small bags.

Large artwork or mirrors hung in a small entryway can make it feel much larger.

Create a Cozy Entryway

If your small hallway feels cold, you can warm it up and make it functional with a shallow bench placed along the longest wall. The bench can help control clutter and helps get you out the door faster because you can store shoes, bags, or jackets underneath. Putting a seat cushion in a colorful fabric on top of the bench will add texture and make the space more inviting and cozy. You can also mount a long plaque of coat hooks on the wall above the bench to hold purses, backpacks, and jackets.

A drop-leaf table that folds to 14 inches fits perfectly in an entryway and adds character to the space. Keep the leaves folded down for everyday use. When you entertain, you can lift one leaf and create a bar, or you can move the table, raise both sides of the leaves, and let it double as your dining table.

Another way to add storage to your hallway is to line it with 12-inch-deep, floor-to-ceiling bookcases. You'll still have room to pass through the hall, but you'll gain tons of storage in a space that's often underutilized. Plus, it's a great place to have your library and will help create a cozy atmosphere. The different colors of the book spines will add dimension, and you can consider lighting up the shelves with track lights or mounted picture lights.

Above: You don't need a deep unit in your entry, just something that has storage and allows you to set items down when you walk in.

Above right: A tall bookcase is great in a hallway—just make sure the shelving is open and not closed in; that way light can still pass through, which will give the entryway a more open feeling.

Cut into your walls to create niche spaces, or alcoves, which are set back and thus don't impose on the footprint of the space. Alcoves can be illuminated to become little display areas for art and objects.

If you have niches and you can light them, they'll add a soft glow and make your hallway feel much larger by adding another layer of light.

148

Above left: Mixing glass and silver items in this niche reflect light and brighten up what would otherwise be a dark little spot.

Above right: When styling niches, don't be afraid to mix art pieces with vases that will keep it from looking too stiff.

Left: If you have very shallow recessed niches in your hallway, it might be a good opportunity to display some collectables rather than letting them take up valuable tabletop space. If you light them with track lights, it can create a special feeling to your entry.

LIBBY'S TRICKS OF THE TRADE

Get the Hang of It—
How to Install Art in Your Home

I knew these frames were going to be arranged around a large flat-screen TV, so in the store I laid them all out on the floor to make sure I had the right quantities and configurations. This was also going to let me know how many vertical and horizontal images I'd need and the sizes of each.

Once they were all framed, I set them on the floor to make sure I liked the layout; it's always better to check it on the floor first instead of turning your wall into a pincushion.

When it comes to artwork in your small space, be sure to THINK BIG! Artwork in a space is really the finishing touch, an element that instantly creates warmth, a point of interest, and something that can visually expand a room. Here I want to share a few tricks I know on how to successfully incorporate art into a room and the best way to hang it!

- Install your artwork so that the picture's center point rests at eye level for the average person.

- When you're installing more than one piece of art (in a grouping), remember to think of it as one unit. Before you start pounding nails into the wall, arrange the artwork on the floor—or, better yet, lay out each piece on brown wrapping paper, trace it, and cut the paper along the traced lines. Then look at the back of each piece to determine where the picture-hanging hook

will go. Next, tape the cut pieces of paper to the wall to help you determine how to group them together, as well as where to place each picture-hanging hook. This process gives you an idea of what the artwork will look like on your wall and makes the installation a snap!

- If you need to hang a grouping of pictures all at the same height (as you'd see in a gallery), hold one of the frames up on the wall at the desired height and mark the wall at the top of the frame. Next, use a measuring tape and measure the space between the mark on the wall and the ceiling; note this measurement, because you'll want all the pictures to hang this same distance down from the ceiling. Now measure the area on the back of the artwork between the top of the frame and the actual picture-hanging wire and add that number to the first number—this will give you the exact placement of where the picture-hanging hook should go in the wall.

This is a great option to downplay the size of a huge wall-mount flat-screen TV. By hanging pictures all the way around it, you deflect the focus from just the TV to some interesting family photos.

• As a general rule, when hanging art over a piece of furniture, the art shouldn't be more than 75 percent of the furniture's width. It should be as tall as possible in a small space, however, because this will make the room feel so much larger. I prefer to have the bottom of the artwork begin about 7 to 10 inches from the top of the furniture below.

• Artwork with horizontal lines will elongate or widen a wall. It will also draw attention to the focal part of the room. Artwork with vertical lines adds to the illusion of height in a room.

• Always use picture-hanging hooks rated for the weight of the art (5 pounds, 20 pounds, 100 pounds). And

when hanging heavier items, such as large mirrors, be sure to use anchors that go into the wall. You want them to be as secure and supported as possible!

• Artwork can be lost visually unless it's properly illuminated. By putting the right light on your art, you can make it feel much more important. You'll also make your room look larger by adding an additional layer of light.

Epilogue
The Grand Finale!

All right, thanks for reading (and if you just looked at the pictures, that's totally cool too!). I hope I've given you some innovative ideas, inspiration, and initiative to start working on your space and transforming it into the home you've always wanted or dreamed of, no matter the size. It's no mistake that the cliché "Home is where the heart is" has withstood the test of time; it's so true that our surroundings support us, shape our views, and color our moods. Our personal spaces are a reflection of who we are, what feels comfortable to us, and the life we want to lead. Our homes are the gifts that give back no matter how long or hard our day has been, what disasters have popped up, or what uncertainties may lie ahead. Your space should welcome you at the end of the day and say, "Hello friend, I'm glad you're back." I hope I've given you some insight on how to *make your space a place you really want to come home to!*

Appendix

Libby's Greatest Color Hits
Paint Color-Ways
The following color groupings work well together for primary colors and accents:

Gold/Red/Black			
Aqua/White/Chocolate			
Ice Blue/Tan/White			
Russet/Tan/Black			
Mauve/Chocolate/White			
Sage/White/Chocolate			
Gray/Cream/Black			
Citron/Black/White			
Navy/White/Tan			
Maroon Brown/Tan/White			
Orange/Black/White			

Best Paint and Wood Color Combinations

The following examples reveal the best paint color to pair with different types of wood. Whether with your floors or furniture, certain colors balance and complement different wood tones.

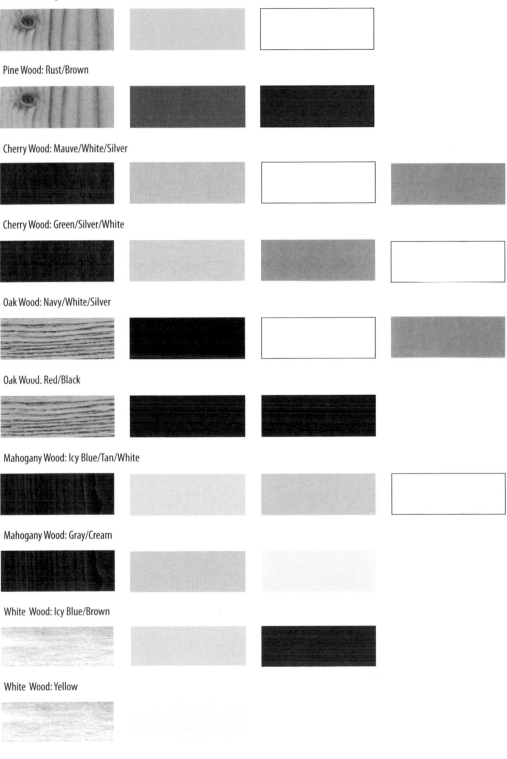

Pine Wood: Sage Green/White

Pine Wood: Rust/Brown

Cherry Wood: Mauve/White/Silver

Cherry Wood: Green/Silver/White

Oak Wood: Navy/White/Silver

Oak Wood: Red/Black

Mahogany Wood: Icy Blue/Tan/White

Mahogany Wood: Gray/Cream

White Wood: Icy Blue/Brown

White Wood: Yellow

Pickled Wood: Aqua/White

Black Wood: Gray/Cream

Libby's Low-Commitment Color Hits

Incorporate the following items into your design as accent pieces. They provide a quick color hit and can easily be replaced when you want a change!

Vases	Throw blanket	Throw pillows	Small ottomans
Candlesticks	Plates	Shower curtain	Towels
Drapes	Picture frames	Small planters	Bedding/dust skirt

Libby's Glossary of Design Terms

Accent lighting: A light that is controlled and directed to highlight or focus attention on a specific design element—for example, a picture light or track light directed onto artwork.

Alcove: A nook or niche that is recessed yet still part of a larger space; it's usually closed in on three sides and often has a ceiling that's a little lower than the space it's attached to. Alcoves are great for offices and intimate dining areas.

Ambient light: The amount of overall light that's in a space, whether from natural sunlight or artificial ceiling light. You want to combine this general light with accent lighting. Multiple layers of light give small spaces a larger feeling.

Asymmetrical: When items are not equally balanced and placed off center to one another, they are asymmetrical. For example, instead of balancing one candlestick on each end of your mantle, the asymmetrical positioning would be to place three candlesticks on one end and some books and a plant on the other . . . I'm totally asymmetrical!

Backsplash: The vertical area above a counter, often found behind a sink and under wall-mount kitchen cabinets, anywhere from 3 inches high up to 24 inches high. Backsplashes are sometimes tiled or covered with a water-resistant material, because their purpose is to shield the wall space from water that could splash up from the sink.

Banquette: A solid built-in or freestanding upholstered bench with an attached upright back. Banquettes are often used in restaurants, but they are a great solution in a small dining area, because storage can be built into the base of the bench.

Baseboard: A section of trim where the wall meets the floor. It adds a finished look and can be made out of wood, vinyl, or even a sturdy foamlike material. It's often painted a different color from the walls (or at least it should be!)

Batting: Thin layers of cotton or poly fibers, usually about 1 inch thick, that are used for wrapping cushions, quilting, and making crafts. It's also used as an underlayer if you are covering your walls in fabric; it adds a soundproofing element as well as a smooth surface.

Beveled edge: An angled, slanted-edge detail used primarily on mirrors and glass. A bevel can come in sizes from ¼ inch up to 1 inch and adds a finished look.

Binding: A piece of fabric sewn to the edge of an area rug that keeps it from fraying. It's the perfect solution if you want to create an area rug out of wall-to-wall carpeting; by binding the edges, you can choose your own custom size.

Bolster: A cylindrical-shaped pillow that usually goes with other decorative pillows on a bed. Sometimes the ends are gathered and tied up (think Tootsie Roll). They can also be placed along the side arms of a sofa for visual interest.

Cafe curtain: A window treatment that only covers the bottom half of a window. It can easily be installed with a tension rod on the inside casing of a window. It's good for small spaces, because the lower covered area gives you privacy while the upper open area still lets in natural light.

Case goods: Furniture pieces that are made mostly of wood, such as end tables, dining tables, dressers, and shelving units, versus upholstered items that are usually covered in fabric, such as sofas, ottomans, or chairs.

Casing: The trim around a window or door opening.

Chair rail: A piece of wood trim attached horizontally on the walls around a room. The wood piece is about 4 inches high and is mounted on the wall about 30 inches up off the floor. It's used to visually scale down large walls, but it is a great opportunity to break up the look of a room by painting the area above a different color from the area below or adding wallpaper to just the upper or lower area.

Chenille: A soft fabric that has some qualities of velvet. It's fuzzy and often used on sofas. Chenille wears well and is incredibly comfortable.

Color scheme: The qualities of the color you choose for a room or project—for example: light, dark, colorful.

Color way: Multiple color combinations for the same pattern of fabric, carpeting, wallpaper, and so on. One floral fabric pattern comes in a red/yellow version, blue/green version and purple/pink version; or I also talk about color ways in the specific colors you choose for a space. For example, the color way for your bedroom may be aqua, gray, and white.

Console table: A long, narrow table usually placed behind a sofa or along an entryway wall. Console tables

often have open shelving units or an open space below, which can be used for additional storage, and the narrow profile doesn't take up too much space.

Contemporary: Designs and furniture pieces that have sleek, simple lines, curves, and geometric patterns. Don't be afraid to mix contemporary pieces with traditional pieces . . . create your own personal style!

Crown molding: Trim molding that's mounted where the ceiling meets the wall. It can also be mounted on top of case goods such as armoires, shelving units, and curio cabinets.

Cubic area: This space equals the length x width x height.

Cylindrical: A round tube-like shape; often this shape can look a bit more contemporary in vases, lamp shades, or table bases.

Damask: A woven fabric, usually a blend of cotton, linen, rayon, or silk, that has both a shiny and matte look to it. Often damask comes in a floral motif and is considered a more traditional-style fabric, but you can also find them in more updated graphic patterns, and the mix of shiny and matte textures adds depth to a small space.

Depth: In literal terms, depth is just the measurement from front to back of any object. In the book I refer

to depth as more of a visual trick: If you can trick the eye into thinking there's more depth in your space than there really is, then you make it appear larger; you can do this with color, lighting, and texture.

Design scheme: Your game plan; your overall design; what you want your space to look like.

Dhurrie rug: A flat, woven area rug from India; they often come in bold colors as well as large graphic patterns. Using a large graphic—patterned rug in a small space can make it look larger; you just need to make sure the rug is big enough for your space . . . no wimpy rugs!

Dimension: Quite simply, the height, width, and depth of an object or your overall space. I refer to dimension in the book (often paired with *depth)* as a visual tool to make it appear that you have more square footage than you really do. I also use it in conjunction with proportion—using items that are the right dimensions and proportions for your space can make it look bigger than it is.

Dimmer switch: A slide switch or turn knob that allows you to control the level of electric lighting, such as in chandeliers, recessed cans, and wall sconces. Dimmer switches are your friends! They allow one fixture to be all things to all people; turn your chandelier lights up all the way when the kids are doing homework and turn it way down when you are hosting a dinner party.

Distressed: A finish on furniture that's made to look aged and worn. Some people think of distressed as damaged, but it's really meant to give the casual feeling of "Come on in, relax, and put your feet up."

Door surround: The trim pieces around a doorway or door casing. You want to measure the inside section of this before you buy that humongous sofa, so you can be sure it will fit through the door!

Double faced: Two layers of fabric sewn or bound together, which allows them to be reversible. When using curtain panels as a way to divide a room, you want to make sure that they are double faced to look great both coming and going! Also, you don't always have to sew the same fabric on both sides; you can break it up to add different looks in each area the curtain panels face.

Double-hung windows: A single window opening that has two window sections that slide past each other in a track to open. Small kitchens often have double-hung windows, and you can mount glass shelves in front of them to hold specialty glassware and stemware. You'll gain lots of storage, but the natural light will still shine through the glassware.

Down light: A light source that faces down from the ceiling. The more you can control a down light to aim towards a specific point in your room, the more effective they'll be. Whether you want to illuminate a piece of artwork, a display cabinet, or a work area, angle your lights and put them to work!

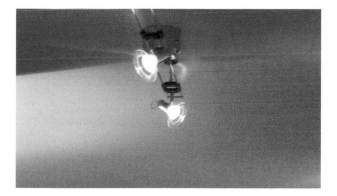

Eclectic: Incorporating styles and design elements from lots of different eras and sources. Eclectic is me giving you permission to mix that southwestern coffee table you've loved forever with the groovy 1950s orange sofa you've just fallen in love with; it's mixing and matching different genres of design to create your own look.

Element: An individual aspect or object that's part of your *design scheme*. In the book, I refer to the elements of color, accessories, and furniture—basically anything you choose that's going into your space when it's all said and done. When all the elements come together, your design takes shape.

Elevation: A scaled drawing that shows details of interior or exterior walls. This is different from a *layout*, which is typically showing you the overhead view of your room. The elevation shows you exactly what's on any given wall as if you were standing in the room looking at it.

Enamel: A hard painted finish on a surface that ranges from low luster to high gloss. It could be on a floor, side table, or picture frame, but the high-shine finish bounces light around a small space and makes it seem bigger.

Étagère: A tall open shelving unit used to display objects or books. I included this here because inevitably when you are shopping for furniture on the Internet, they mention étagères. They are such an important element in any small room and can be put to use in myriad ways that I don't want you to skip over them!

Ethnic: Patterns and styles influenced by the cultures of other regions. Ethnicity is important, because if you want a specific look, such as an African, Moroccan, or an Asian design style, you can communicate the message to a salesperson or look for stores that feature ethnic styles and you'll be more likely to find exactly what you want!

Euro shams: These 26-inch square pillows with decorative sham covers are most commonly combined with other pillows on beds. The Euro shams are the largest pillows you can find and are great as an alternative to a headboard; three placed side-by-side and positioned against the wall a bed is on have enough height to spiff up any plain-Jane bedroom.

Exotic: Unique, dramatic elements native to another country. In design, *exotic* is a specific item and often related to an animal—a zebra-print rug or a snakeskin-patterned wallpaper—whereas *ethnic* is the overall look and feel of a room.

Fiberboard: A board made of compressed wood shavings and glue. Fiberboard is not expensive; it's relatively lightweight, and it's easy enough to staple items into it. It's great to use if you want to upholster your own headboard, seat cushions, window seats, or bench cushions. It's easy to wrap batting around fiberboard, cover both with fabric, and then staple gun it all together on the underside of the fiberboard.

Finial: A metal or wood decorative cap used on the end of drapery rods, the top of a lamp to secure the shade, or on the tops of bedposts.

Finishes: Final stains, paints, coatings, or treatments used on various furniture surfaces. Finishes relate to items I've discussed in regard to paint and wood color combinations as well as matte versus high-gloss finishes.

Floor plan: A scaled drawing that usually shows ¼ inch equal to 1 foot. Floor plans show the overhead view of walls and the placement of windows, doors, and electrical outlets. A floor plan is what you need to create (or get from your builder/landlord) in order to decide on the best possible furniture placement in your space. A *layout* is what a floor plan looks like when all the furniture is added and placed in your space.

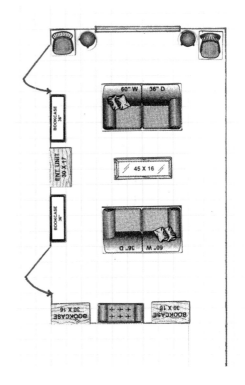

Foam core board: A stiff sheet of Styrofoam with laminated paper on the front and back. This stuff is great if you are making your own corkboard or hanging organizer for a wall. It's lightweight and can be wrapped in fabric and attached to a wall as a stylish, inexpensive note holder.

Focal point: A specific visual element in a room that becomes the main focus of the space. A fireplace, a great view, a wall unit, a piece of artwork, or a piece of furniture can all be the focal point of a room. When I refer to painting an accent wall, it's usually to create a focal point in the room. Creating a focal point, whether using paint, art, or furniture, gives weight and importance to your space and makes it feel larger.

Fullness: The number of fabric widths in drapery treatments and the amount of volume in the drapes. Basically the more fabric you use, the more fullness you have. When using drapes as a divider in a room or to cover a wall of storage, you want to take into account the amount of fullness you'll need to cover the spans of feet from one side to the next; you want to make sure there's enough fabric to cover the overall area.

Furnishings: Artwork, accessories, area rugs, cabinetry, lighting, storage units, window treatments, and upholstery . . . pretty much everything that makes your house feel like a home falls under the category of furnishings.

Gable: Usually in an attic of a house, it's the triangular area that's created by the two sloping rooflines and an end wall. If you have an attic, be sure not to overlook this space—it can often be successfully turned into a home office, a spare sleeping nook, or a craft area.

Geometric: A pattern with simple, linear shapes. Small geometric patterns work well in small spaces on wallpaper, rugs, and fabrics, whereas large geometric patterns might actually make it look smaller.

Giclée: Photographic prints used for wall art. They are created from high-resolution digital images with great detail that have been printed using top-quality ink-jet printers. They are often printed on high-gloss paper and can have a very sleek, modern look. Use these sophisticated prints as inspiration to take your own pictures and print them up and frame them!

Gold leaf: Tissue-thin layers of gold painted onto a prepared adhesive surface. It's used on everything from furniture to picture frames to ceilings. It's great in a small space, because the reflective quality of the gold bounces light around. Remember, though, that a little gold leaf goes a long way, and you don't want to overdo it on too many items.

Grommet: Two round metal sleeves crimped together to strengthen a hole, most often in fabric. Grommets are often used on the holes on the tops of shower curtains. They can also be used on the tops of drapery panels and work well if you are mounting your drapes from a track on the ceiling.

Header or Heading: The finished section on the top of a drapery panel that accommodates the drapery pole, rings, clips, or grommets.

Head rail: The horizontal bar and section that hides and houses window-blind mechanisms. In a small space I recommend ordering blinds longer than your windows so the head rail can be mounted up near the ceiling; this will draw your eye upward and make your ceiling seem higher and your room bigger.

Hue: A specific aspect of a color based on the dark and light qualities it has. There are many different hues in the color spectrum of red, blue, green, and yellow. For example, a bright cherry red is a completely different hue of red than a dark brick red.

Incandescent light: Lighting from a conventional light bulb or halogen bulb, incandescent light has bright white, clear qualities, whereas fluorescent light has a blue green quality to it.

Inside mount: Installation of a window covering inside the actual window-frame casing. In a small space this isn't as good as mounting the window shade outside your window frame—you don't want the blind to block any natural light.

Jamb: The interior sides of a door or a window frame. Be sure to measure this dimension before purchasing any large items of furniture, such as armoires, sofas, or dressers, to be sure that they will fit through the doorway.

Key pattern: A classical decorative pattern made up of angular, geometric, and symmetrical designs, sometimes interlocking and overlapping lines. Many times key patterns are used as borders in rugs, shower curtains, drapes, and bedding. And if you want pattern in your space, but don't want a busy all-over pattern, key patterns can work well as a happy medium.

Kick plate: A protective plate mounted to the bottom of a door to protect it from wear and tear.

Kilim: Handwoven rugs from the Middle East that have geometric designs. They come in dark rich color ways, but they are also available in paler, softer color ways—which may be a better choice to make your small space feel larger.

Lacquer: A synthetic coating that's dried to form a protective, high-gloss film. Lacquer is great on furniture, picture frames, and accessories in small spaces, because the shiny finish looks sleek and reflects light.

Lattice: A crisscross pattern on fabrics, wall coverings, and rugs. This pattern is great in small spaces, because it tricks the eye and makes an area feel larger. Lattice works on the diagonal, which visually elongates an area.

Loveseat: A smaller version of a sofa, usually meant to seat two people (a sofa is meant to seat three). No more than two people ever really sit on a full sofa anyway, so I recommend loveseats as a way to have a smaller sofa and free up room for more occasional chairs or end tables.

Matelasse: Fabric intricately woven in a double weave, which gives it the slight appearance of being quilted or embossed. It's mostly used in bedding, is often a solid color, and has a great lightweight texture.

Mattes or Matte board: Thin cardboard with a decorative paper or fabric applied to the surface and used when framing pictures or artwork to keep it from touching the glass. Using mattes even with store-bought frames can give a more expensive, custom look for not much money!

Monochromatic: All the hues and shades of just one color, ranging from dark to light.

Murphy bed: A mattress and frame that fold down or are raised into a concealed wall cabinet or built-in unit.

Nail-head trim: An upholstery detail using decorative metal tacks as a finish trim on the edging of chairs, ottomans, and sofas. Nail-head tacks are a great tool in a small space. They can hold fabric on walls and corkboards and add an interesting detail to an upholstered headboard. They are sturdier and larger than regular tacks and come in several different sizes and metal finishes.

Niche: A recessed opening, often arched at the top, set into a wall with a shelf and sometimes lit from the top to showcase a display or art object. Niches are invaluable in a small bathroom, hallway, living room, or kitchen—they are nooks that can store items and don't eat into the square footage of the room.

Occasional furniture: You're probably thinking what in the world does this mean . . . if it's only occasionally furniture, what is it the rest of the time? This is a generic term that refers to smaller pieces of furniture that complement the main pieces. For example, in a living room the main piece would be a sofa, and an accent chair or ottoman would be the occasional pieces. It's a good idea in a small space to keep the fabrics on larger pieces neutral, textured, or solid and have more fun with bolder and printed fabrics on the occasional furniture.

Occasional tables: A generic term used for any small table (not a dining table or coffee table).

Opaque: A surface or material that does not allow light to pass through, such as blackout shades.

Ottoman: An upholstered furniture piece used as a stool, footrest, or coffee table. I find ottomans to be incredibly useful in a myriad of ways in a small space.

Outside mount: Installation of window coverings mounted on the wall beyond the window frame. I prefer this method to the *inside mount* to make a small space feel bigger.

Overscale: Large in scale or size for the space. Overscale lamps, rugs, and artwork help make a small room seem larger, whereas overscale furniture might actually make it feel smaller.

Padding: Fabric or materials used to provide extra cushioning; see *batting*.

Parquet: Wood flooring laid in geometric patterns.

Pattern repeat: Increments between vertical or horizontal patterns repeated in fabric and wall coverings. The pattern repeat can be important if you are upholstering a headboard with a patterned fabric—you want to make sure it is balanced with the same amount of pattern on one side as the other.

Pendant: A hanging light fixture that's mounted from the ceiling. These are used over kitchen counters to provide direct task lighting. In a small space the pendant shouldn't be too large, or it will visually cut the room in half and make it seem smaller.

Pigment: The actual substance that turns a certain material a certain color.

Pitch: The degree to which a roof slopes, or the angle of a seat back in a chair. The pitch is the difference between a chair that has a straight, upright seat back and a chair that has a seat back that has a more leaned-back position. For everyday use you most likely want a chair with a seat pitch that's right in the middle, not too far up and not too far back.

Pocket door: An interior door on a track that slides into a wall. If your walls are thick enough and do not have support beams, you may be a candidate for pocket doors. Pocket doors are great because you don't have to allow the clearance space for the door to open into the room.

Primary color: Red, yellow, and blue as the basis for all other colors on the color wheel—these colors come before the *secondary* and *tertiary* colors.

Recessed light: A lighting fixture installed up in the ceiling.

Repeat: The vertical or horizontal measurements for a patterned woven or printed fabric; it's the distance from a point in a pattern to the same point where the pattern starts again.

Riser: The vertical section of a staircase that supports the horizontal *tread.* Often risers can be cut out and drawers can be installed in the cutout to capitalize on storage underneath stairs. Risers can also be painted another color to add visual interest to a small stairwell.

Rod pocket: A stitched pocket or channel that holds a drapery rod.

Roller shade: A flat window treatment, often made from fabric or vinyl, that uses spring rollers inside the window frame to be raised and lowered. Roller shades can be good in small spaces because they roll up nice and tight when they are up, so they are not as noticeable as *Roman shades* and don't block out any natural light. They are also fairly inexpensive.

Roman shade: A window treatment that uses a series of window tapes, rings, and cords stitched to the back side to be raised and lowered; it draws up to horizontal pleats or folds when it's raised. There are different types of Roman shades:

- **Flat Roman:** When fully extended this shade is completely flat.

- **Shirred balloon shade:** This shade has unstructured poufs of fabric gathered or *shirred* at the top.
- **Soft-fold Roman:** When fully extended this shade keeps soft folds down the full length of the shade (this one requires more fabric).

Saturation: In colors—this refers to the concentration of a *hue,* so highly saturated colors are vibrant and low-saturated colors are muted. Highly saturated colors work well for accessories, accent walls, and spots where you want punches of bright color. Low-saturated colors work well on larger pieces of upholstery, because they are more muted and won't look too busy.

Scale: A drafting increment used to measure distances and relationships between the amount of square footage and the sizes of the architectural and interior details in a room. The increment most commonly used is ¼-inch scale, which means on a *layout* or an *elevation,* ¼ inch equals 1 foot. This makes it easier when you want an entire room layout to fit on one piece of paper.

Sconce: A wall-mounted electric light fixture.

Screen: Multiple hinged panels that can stand in a zigzag configuration; they are often made from wood, fabric panels, or iron. Screens are great room dividers for small spaces, particularly if they are made from a translucent material that allows natural light to pass through.

Secondary color: The blend of two *primary colors* on the color wheel—green, orange, and purple are secondary colors.

Serging: A sewing finishing technique in which you oversew the raw edge of a carpet. It is primarily used when you take a piece of wall-to-wall carpet (or a remnant) and have it cut and bound to fit your room. It's the most inexpensive way to do it, and you get a great look!

Sheers: A window treatment made with translucent fabric and material.

Shirred curtain: A window treatment that's gathered onto a drapery rod and bunched together on the rod to form irregular pleats; the drapery *header* would be above the *rod pocket.*

Sidelight: Stationary vertical windows that flank both sides of an entry door; they are usually tall and skinny.

Sisal: A strong natural fiber made from sisal leaves woven together to create a floor covering. It's a "beachy," casual look but should not be used when you're looking for a rug that you want to be soft underfoot (such as in the bedroom, bathroom, or living room), as they are often a little more scratchy than fiber rugs.

Slipper chair: An *occasional* chair that's armless, usually with a skirt to the floor and low to the ground. Slipper chairs are typically used in the bedroom because of their smaller size, but they are also a great choice in a small living room because of their *scale*.

Soffit: The underside of a structural section in a room, usually up at the ceiling, a soffit is a dropped section or overhang. Consider hanging a shelf up along your entire soffit to display books and art objects that you don't need to access frequently. It's a great use of usually wasted space and can visually make your room feel larger.

Space planning: Arranging fixtures and furnishings in a space, taking into account traffic flow, furniture scale, number of occupants—basically finding the most efficient use for you and all your belongings in the space you have.

Spring-tension rod: An adjustable drapery rod that contains an inner spring/coil system that allows you to tightly compress the rod and then put it into a window frame or opening. They also come as adjustable-tension rods, so you set them into the opening you want, with the drapes shirred on them, and twist the rods until there's enough tension to hold the rod in place between a door or window frame. These are a great choice for renters who can't drill into a wall; they're quick, inexpensive, and easy! They also work well in closet door openings if you want fabric panels instead of closet doors.

Square feet: Width times length measured in feet (2 feet by 2 feet equals 4 square feet; 3 feet by 3 feet equals 9 square feet), often abbreviated to sq. ft.

Square yard: Width times length measured in *yards* (2 *yards* x 2 *yards* equals 4 square *yards*), often abbreviated to sq. yd.

Stack back: The amount of space needed on either side of working drapery panels when they are completely open. I prefer for drapes to stack on the wall rather than inside the window frame when they are open; this gives the illusion of a larger window and keeps the drapes from blocking out natural light.

Symmetrical: Matching designs placed opposite one another. Some people are very symmetrical; they want complete and utter balance—if there's a plant at one end of the table, then they want a second plant just like it at the opposite end of the table. I'm more asymmetrical and prefer not to be quite so evenly balanced.

Swag: Fabric that curves between two points, these are often used to go over a drapery rod and can have a more traditional look.

Table runner: A slim, long decorative cloth, usually running lengthwise down the center of a dining table. These can look great if you use a fabric that contrasts with the *finish* of your dining table, and the long sleek line can elongate the look of your table.

Tabletop: The top surface of your table, which can be made of wood, glass, stone, or any manmade materials. There are several edge finishes that you can choose from for your tabletop:

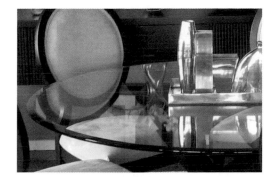

- **Beveled:** A slanted edge with a square bottom.
- **Bull nose:** A thick round edge, like a half-moon shape.
- **Flat:** A straight cut.
- **Eased:** A straight cut with the corners softened or eased just slightly.
- **Radius:** A slightly rounded top.

Tailored: A neat custom-fit look; not slouchy, oversize, or overstuffed. Tailored furniture is a great choice for a small space; the clean, crisp lines feel controlled yet comfortable.

Taper: A gradual transition often referred to in the context of chair or table legs. Tapered legs are larger at the top and then taper down to a smaller leg at the bottom.

Task lighting: Lighting required for work activities or things that require visual attention, such as a reading lamp or *pendant* fixtures over a kitchen counter.

Tertiary color: A *primary* and *secondary* color on the color wheel blended together. Red orange, blue green, yellow green, and blue violet are tertiary colors.

Texture: The overall intertwined structure of fabrics, carpeting, or any material in a space. Textures come in various feels—everything from burlap to velvet to sea grass to silk; these are all textures that can add *depth* and *dimension* to a space!

Throw: A small decorative blanket or spread. There are also throw pillows, which are decorative pillows.

Tieback: A decorative hook or fabric tie used to hold drapery panels away from the center of a window.

Tone: A tint or shade of color.

Tone on tone: Using two or more shades of the same *hue.* Tan tone-on-tone silk-striped drapery panels would be made of fabric that has stripes out of a light tan as well as stripes that are a darker tan; they are both tans, but one is lighter than the other.

Torchiere: A standing floor lamp that gives off indirect upward light. I'm putting this in here because I really *don't like* these lamps. I think they give off a cold, uninviting quality of light. Instead I'd recommend an *incandescent* floor lamp with a nice *sheer* lamp shade.

Transitional: A general style that is right between traditional and modern. The majority of people prefer a transitional style; it's very comfortable yet chic.

Translucent: A semi-*opaque* surface that diffuses light while partially blocking a view, such as frosted glass or *sheers.*

Transom: A narrow horizontal window placed over a doorway to let in natural light; it's often used in conjunction with *sidelights* over an exterior door. These can be used over interior doors in small spaces to allow light to pass through and to make the space feel larger.

Traverse rod: A cord-controlled drapery rod used for opening and closing window treatments.

Tread: The flat horizontal top area of a staircase; it rests on the *riser.*

Trellis: A combination of horizontal and vertical wood elements constructed to form a *lattice.* It's designed to support vines and climbing outdoor plants, but when you bring a trellis indoors it can make an interesting design element in your small space as well as give you places to insert pegs to hang purses, jackets, and items in an entryway.

Tromp l'oeil: Meaning "fool the eye," this is a painting technique that makes use of shading and highlighting to create three-dimensional, architectural effects. It's often used to make it look as though something's there when it really isn't. An example would be painting a series of lines where a wall meets the ceiling to look as though there's crown molding. Usually this technique is reserved for artists, but it can be achieved by a layperson and is a great way to add depth and the illusion of more space. It's worth investigating to see if it's something you could pull off!

Trundle bed: A twin-size daybed that has an additional mattress below, which can be pulled out when needed. Often the lower mattress sits in a drawer, which is what is pulled out; you may not need the mattress, but the extra storage drawer below is always welcome in a small space.

Tufted: A style or pattern of upholstery that uses knots or buttons that are tightly secured in a pattern over foam or *batting,* which then creates several puffy clusters. The method of tufting is used in everything from upholstered headboards and chairs to upholstered ottomans.

Under-counter lighting: Lights mounted underneath wall cabinets to provide additional *task lighting* to the countertops.

Uplight: Light that shines up from the floor and is usually facing toward and illuminating an object. Often you'll see can uplights shining up on tall floor plants.

Valance: A shallow drapery treatment placed at the *heading* of a window, hiding the hardware and pull mechanism underneath it.

Veneer: Paper-thin wood sheets applied to the outer surface of furniture. Often veneer is used to manufacture less-expensive *case goods.* The main construction of the piece is built from plywood or less-expensive material, and then a veneer of more-expensive wood is glued to the top and finished to create the desired look. Furniture using veneer isn't a bad thing, and when you are just starting out it's most likely what you'll be able to afford; don't sweat it, you have the rest of your life to be able to collect expensive furniture. For now, get your place looking good!

Wainscoting: Material, usually wood, that's applied to the bottom third of an interior wall; some examples are bead board and paneling below a *chair rail.* It can also be applied to just the upper section of a wall, which can give a more classic country look.

Wall hanging: A tapestry, or bound piece of fabric, hung on the wall, often from an iron drapery rod. These are great behind sofas or hung from the ceiling over a bed and then down the wall behind the bed. They can create a *focal point* in a room.

Welt: Fabric-wrapped cording that's used to reinforce as well as decorate seams in upholstery. I love contrast welt—that's when a sofa fabric is one color but the seam has a welt that's another color. It's an added touch that offers a big punch of style.

Width: In fabric this refers to one strip of material of any length; upholstery fabric is usually about 54 inches wide, so that means one width is 54 inches.

Yard: The unit most often used to measure fabric; I yard is equal to 3 feet or 36 inches.

Acknowledgments

I'd like to thank...

Photographer **Noël Sutherland** for his gifted eye and astonishing talent in seeing things that other people truly cannot see. I'm blessed that he maintained his relentless pursuit of photo perfection even when I was standing behind him saying "Hurry up." I always love it when I can feel him on the other side of the lens; he's an incredible friend and makes photo shoots fun with his excitement and never-ending library of new music. **www.noelsutherland.com.**

Morris Reid for starting on this journey with me, listening to my five-year-plan and rolling up his sleeves to help me accomplish all that I could in that time.

Carol Mann, my book agent, for her belief in this book and all things "Libby."

Laura Yorke for helping me take the writing blob I started with and organizing it into a perfect book proposal. She helped position the book in just the right way, and for that I will be forever grateful!

Keith O'Hea for his unconditional support, love, and encouragement throughout the entire writing process, for graciously and patiently allowing me to write all weekend, never saying a word, and for acting as my adorable, human thesaurus.

Lara Asher, my editor, for reading the proposal and deciding this would be a good book to publish. I've always felt her enthusiasm throughout this process and cannot thank her enough for her energy and hard work in helping to champion my small-space message. I hope this is the first of many books that we work on together. She made it a safe place for me to write what I wanted and encouraged me to put my voice and my wacky personality down on paper.

Lauren Hooper for being the quiet giant who keeps everything moving on the "Libby Train." Her willingness to do whatever needs to be done is always appreciated, and her dynamic energy and hard work are a constant. She is also an incredible source of support, gives great feedback, and is tireless at making things happen when they need to. Beyond all she does for me, she is also an incredible person with an amazing soul and someone I'm lucky to call a friend . . . she makes the office a fun place to work every day.

Sonja Olson for taking my first gazillion pages of ideas and tips and helping me organize them so I could see what I really had to start with.

Rebecca Ahrens for helping with the photo layouts for the book proposal; she worked to make it look appealing, informative, and full of style.

Regina Von Schack for helping with the photo shoots in New York City and Sag Harbor. She just jumped in and did whatever needed to be done, and her ability to style was definitely needed and much appreciated.

The wonderful team at Globe Pequot Press for their focus and creativity and for taking this book and treating it like it's their baby! **Jenn Taber, Cynthia Hughes, Sheryl Kober,** and **Georgiana Goodwin.**

The GPP sales team for working hard to get this book into as many hands as possible and thinking outside of the box on how to achieve that! **Michelle Lewy, John Groton, Chris Grimm,** and **Amy Alexander.**

The GPP marketing and PR team for their effort and energy to shout out my small space message from the rooftops! **Inger Forland, Bob Sembiante,** and **John Spalding.**

Brian O'Hea and **Carlos Hatch** for sharing their gorgeous small space with me and allowing us to photograph it. Their space is everything they are all about: witty, chic, and elegant, and I thank them for letting me offer that to readers as beautiful design inspiration.

Melanie Mintz and **Christina Scott** for letting us shoot in the two incredibly fabulous and functional small spaces they designed. The apartments oozed style as well as efficiency and proved that you can think big even in a tiny place. **Melanie Mintz Design** with Christina Scott, (917) 204-1177.

Christina Scott of Metropolitan Decorating for allowing me to photograph her beautiful interior design work in a small apartment, her talent is creating gorgeous spaces that can truly be lived in and enjoyed. I also thank her for styling the space to photo-ready perfection! metropolitandecorating.com; (202) 465-1816.

Patricia Fox for allowing me to photograph her gorgeous jewel box of an apartment; her rich, luxurious interior design style is felt in every detail in her space, and I'm thrilled to showcase her signature sassy and savvy look. Her generous spirit was amazing when we were shooting, and it really was one of our favorite afternoons! I also thank her for my special signs that are hanging in my kitchen, "I'm So Lucky" and "Don't Forget to Eat!" **www.patriciafoxdesign.com,** (646) 209-3600.

Carla Holtze for sharing her space as well as offering design inspiration from her worldly travels.

Debbie and **John Loeffler** for their friendship and permission to showcase their beautiful home; I adored working with them and I thank Kitty as well!

Jeffrey Moses for giving me the design ball and letting me run with it; he's so much fun to design for and I truly thank him for letting me use images of his gorgeous homes.

Dory and **Brad Faxon** for allowing me to use photos of their house; I loved working with them, they are great friends, and their home is a true reflection of their generous spirit.

Colleen and **Joe Ogilvie** for taking a chance on a crazy designer from New York; I had a blast working with them and I so appreciate their sharing pictures of their stunning house with the readers.

Amanda and **Justin Leonard** for the chance to design such a fabulous home and get to know their fantastic family, and for allowing me to offer a glimpse inside it.

Braxton Culler Inc. for allowing me to photograph so many pieces of their beautiful furniture in their High Point, North Carolina showroom. Their stylish and comfortable designs are sure to inspire readers to turn their home into a chic haven. **www .braxtonculler.com**

Peppe Iuele, Pino Coladonato, Enzo Ruggiero, Eddie Ricci Jr., Janet and **Eddie Ricci** for being the first people to take a chance on me as a designer as well as for their incredible friendship. **La Masseria** is the ultimate clubhouse and I love them all!

Dan Wolman and **Massimo Bizzocchi** for their complete faith in me as a designer and for letting me use pictures of their special store in the book. They are the chicest men I know!

Frank, Julie, Anne, HC, Michael, Kelly, Alex, Jordan, Morgan, Dillon, Liam, O'Malley, and **Declan** for laughing with and loving me!

Index

Libby Langdon

Libby Langdon is an interior designer and expert commentator on HGTV's hit show *Small Space, Big Style*. She offers insights, techniques, and tips to help viewers make the most of their own small space. Previously, Libby hosted and was the lead designer on the FOX makeover TV show, *Design Invasion*.

Libby founded Libby Interiors in 2003 and has completed numerous commercial and residential design projects all over the country. She designed the New York City restaurant La Masseria, which was voted as one of the top ten new restaurants in the United States by *Esquire*. She also designed the flagship store for Italian designer Massimo Bizzocchi in New York's Meatpacking District.

Libby has designed private residences in New York's Sagaponack, East Hampton and Southampton, and several apartments in New York City. She's designed homes for PGA golfers Justin Leonard and Joe Ogilvie in Texas as well as Brad Faxon's waterfront home in Rhode Island. She's designed a loft apartment in Providence, Rhode Island as well as the pro shop of the exclusive Atlantic Golf Club in Bridgehampton, New York. Libby is currently designing a small stone cottage on a vineyard in Italy and an apartment in Manhattan.

Libby's designs have been featured in numerous national shelter magazines and on the covers of *Hamptons Cottages and Gardens* and *Decorating Spaces*. She is a small space expert to *Decorating with Style* and *Budget Decorating*, and her tips and ideas have been featured in publications such as *Better Homes and Gardens*, *Woman's Day*, *Glamour*, and *Cosmopolitan* as well as several other design magazines. Libby regularly gives seminars about design in small spaces to furniture retailers and manufacturers, offering ways to court the small space consumer.

Libby is a regular contributor to the nation's top daily papers with design, food, and entertaining ideas. She splits her time between New York City and Sag Harbor, New York.

For design tips, food and entertaining ideas and all things "Libby" go to www.libbylangdon.com.